A **B**RIDE'S *C*OOKBOOK

By Peggy Harvey

WHEN THE COOK'S AWAY

SEASON TO TASTE

A BRIDE'S COOKBOOK

A BRIDE'S COOKBOOK

A Kitchen Primer by

PEGGY HARVEY

An Atlantic Monthly Press Book
Little, Brown and Company
Boston — Toronto.

LIBRARY OF CONGRESS CATALOG CARD NO. 62-9553

FIRST EDITION

ATLANTIC–LITTLE, BROWN BOOKS
ARE PUBLISHED BY
LITTLE, BROWN AND COMPANY
IN ASSOCIATION WITH
THE ATLANTIC MONTHLY PRESS

Published simultaneously in Canada
by Little, Brown & Company (Canada) Limited

PRINTED IN THE UNITED STATES OF AMERICA

FOR JUDY RAND

Contents

Preface	ix
Precepts	3
Equipment, Staples and Herbs	6
Brunches, Lunches and Suppers	14
Appetizers and Soups	37
Meat	42
Poultry	70
Fish	86
When the Exchequer Is Low	93
Leftovers	103
Vegetables	116
Salads	136
Desserts	143
Entertaining	163
A Short Bibliography	178
Index	179

Preface

This book has been written with love: love for Judy, who asked for and received it as a wedding present in its original form — a small black notebook filled with typewritten recipes tailored to her tastes; with love for my daughter, who started married life armed with a similar black notebook filled with slightly revised recipes; and with love for cooking and all would-be cooks. In the same way that I was able to help Judy and my daughter, I hope to help all young brides who find themselves suddenly faced with an array of pots and pans and the unfamiliar necessity of cooking. If you have bought this book or if you have received it as a gift, this obviously means you.

I am assuming that you can make fudge, instant coffee and, possibly, chocolate cake from a mix. If you are any more accomplished than that, you belong in a more advanced class. This is a primer. In it I propose to take you by the hand and lead you gently but gaily into the wonderful world of cooking.

I hope that you will read through this book before you start working with it. I don't mean that you should read every recipe but do read the introductions to them, the generalizations about how to shop and the first and last chapters. If you do this, you will absorb, quite painlessly, a great deal of information which will help enormously as you go along.

You will notice that in the early recipes I tell you how to time your cooking in more detail than I do later. This is because I know that you'll catch on.

Don't let the fact that there are menus upset you. You don't have to follow them; they are just suggestions. If you don't like peas, for instance, or if *he* doesn't, have something else. There are plenty of vegetable recipes in the vegetable section. Be sure, though, to pay attention to color and texture when you plan a meal. Don't have everything creamy-white and soft or all red and firm; don't have creamed chicken, mashed potatoes and cauliflower, for example, or rare steak and beets. Actually, it turns out that if foods look attractive together and there is variety in texture, you are apt to have a balanced meal, dietetically speaking. That may sound dull, but it is important.

All the recipes are for two unless I say otherwise. An asterisk beside a cooking procedure or the name of a dish means that it can be found elsewhere in the book. *Look it up in the Index.*

Substitutions can be made in foodstuffs to suit your budget; margarine may be used instead of butter, half-and-half instead of cream, for instance. But don't try short cuts in cooking. Follow the recipe exactly, at least the first time. It has been carefully worked out. If you want to experiment later on, fine.

Before we start, I hope you'll read and heed the few precepts that begin the book. Anyone can learn to cook. Be bold, but don't hurry. Take it easy. It's fun.

A B*RIDE'S* C*OOKBOOK*

Precepts

1. Read a recipe through carefully before shopping for the ingredients and once again before starting to cook.

2. Have all necessary utensils and groceries handy and in plain sight.

3. Start your cooking with the item which will take the longest time; in other words, don't fix the eggs before you start the bacon.

4. Do as much as possible beforehand. For instance, get the parsley cut if you're going to need it; scrub the potatoes for baking or peel them and put them in cold water if they're to be boiled; peel onions, but don't put them in water (they come apart); have salad greens washed and put in the crisper or wrapped in a damp towel and put in the refrigerator; have dessert made, if possible, and coffee ready to make.

5. Wash up as you go along. When a pan has been used, put it right in the sink and fill it with hot water and soap flakes or detergent unless it has had eggs in it; in that case, fill it with cold water. Finish washing these pans as

soon as you have a minute. Have a draining rack on the sink so that you don't have to dry pots and pans, dishes, or even glasses. Glasses washed in detergent, rinsed in hot water, and drained sparkle more than if dried by hand.

6. Don't plan two kinds of food for the oven unless you're sure that there is enough room and that both dishes will require the same temperature.

7. Don't have two sauces at the same meal unless one is a dessert sauce.

8. Serve a light dessert following a heavy meal.

9. Always take meat, poultry, or fish out of the refrigerator for close to an hour before cooking so that it will be at room temperature. Defrost meat, poultry, or fish before using unless it says on the package not to, as in the case of certain fresh frozen shrimp. Meat *can* be cooked frozen, but it takes longer and I don't think that it's nearly as good.

10. Pay attention to oven temperatures and never put anything in a cold oven unless expressly told to do so.

11. Let broiled or roasted meat or poultry sit in a warm place (on the top of the stove or in the turned-off oven) for 10 to 15 minutes after it's done. This distributes the juices throughout and makes poultry easier to carve.

12. Buy the herbs that I suggest, but buy them in small quantities so that they will stay fresh. Don't be afraid to use them, but don't go overboard. Taste as you add them bit by bit. Too much herb flavoring is worse than none at all. If you are cooking something that is not in this book and want to use herbs or if you want to experiment, consult the herb chart. It will tell you what goes with what.

13. It is not extravagant to have some liquor on hand for cooking. You don't use much of it. Have some Amer-

ican dry wines, both red and white, a bottle of Madeira, one of kirsch, one of dry sherry, one of Marsala, one of port and one of dry vermouth. The port and vermouth may be American; the others should be imported. A touch of wine or spirits, when indicated, can make an ordinary dish extraordinary but will not make it taste like a drink.

14. Last, but definitely not least, have plates hot for hot food and cold for cold food.

Equipment, Staples
and Herbs

KITCHEN EQUIPMENT

We'll hope that your friends see this book before they give you a kitchen shower because many of the "musts" are shower-type things. Of course, if you don't get them all for presents, you'll have to shop for them yourself. The luxuries at the end of the list can be collected during the years as presents from you to your kitchen, in the event, that is, that they fail to show up as wedding gifts.

Baster (this looks like a giant medicine dropper)
Steamer (this is perforated aluminum with movable petals;
     it fits any size saucepan and is used for steaming
     vegetables)
Meat grinder
Individual shirred egg dishes (you use these for sea food
     too)

Enamel double boiler, one with a rounded bottom if
    possible

Flour sifter

2 bread pans (not necessarily for bread; for meat loaf
    and pound cake too)

Custard cups

Melon mold, 1½-quart size (this is not to mold melons
    but to make lovely desserts and entrées)

Food mill approximately 8 inches in diameter (to purée
    and strain vegetables and fruit)

Pepper grinder and black peppercorns

Nutmeg grinder (freshly ground nutmeg has much more
    flavor than powdered)

Ricer (put boiled potatoes or carrots through this before
    mashing)

Kitchen scale; up to 10 pounds

Lemon squeezer

2 enamel-lined iron saucepans, small and medium (color-
    ful outside, gray or white inside)

Roasting pan (big enough for a 10-pound turkey — no
    bigger)

Large chopping board

3 chopping bowls, small, medium, and large, with chopper

Rotary egg beater

Nest of aluminum or stainless steel mixing bowls

Iron cocotte or Dutch oven

Colorful ironware casseroles which are at home in the
    oven, on the stove, in the refrigerator, or on the
    table

Shallow, oval casseroles as above for fish and small roasts

Large soup kettle with tight lid for spaghetti (10-quart
    size)

3 skillets, of iron or cast aluminum, small, medium, and large

Assorted wooden spoons, which do not chip enamel pans

Rack containing stainless steel spatula, large spoon, slotted pancake turner, ladle, two-pronged fork, and slotted spoon

Kitchen cutlery: knives, forks, tablespoons, and teaspoons

Knives, all sizes and shapes, preferably French or German carbon steel. These stain, but their sharpness makes them worth the trouble of taking care of them. Wipe them clean after each use.

Wall can opener

Soufflé dishes, 1-quart and 1½-quart sizes (oh yes, you'll make soufflés)

Griddle

Pot holders and mitts

Several asbestos pads (for cooking over low heat and for keeping food warm)

2 colanders, 1 medium and 1 small (for draining vegetables and for keeping them warm over hot water)

Cookie sheet (used for other things besides cookies)

Cheese grater

Garlic press

Measuring cups

Measuring spoons

Skewers

Grapefruit knife

1-quart measure (an enamel pitcher)

Round toothpicks

Plastic containers with tight-fitting lids, preferably square, for refrigerator and freezer

2 strainers, 1 small, 1 medium

Enamel or aluminum saucepans with lids
9-inch pie plate
10-inch cake tin
Wire whisk
Rolling pin
Pastry brush
Cookie cutters, several sizes
Rubber scraper
Apple corer
Vegetable peeler
Vegetable brush
Kitchen tongs
Cake rack
Scoops for potato and melon balls
Shrimp deveiner (Shrimpmaster)
Cheesecloth
Paper towels
Kitchen scissors

Luxuries

Electric mixer with dough hook, wire whisk, puréer, and
        meat grinder attachments
Electric blender
Electric deep fryer
Electric skillet
Rotisserie
Waffle iron

STAPLES YOU SHOULD HAVE

Salt (iodized or not, depending on where you live)
Lawry's Seasoned Salt

Onion salt
Celery salt
Accent or monosodium glutamate
Black peppercorns
White peppercorns
Hungarian paprika
Cayenne pepper
Herbs (see chart)
All-purpose flour (5 pounds)
Cake flour (2 pounds)
Pastry flour (2 pounds)
Double-action baking powder
Olive oil (1 pint)
Peanut oil (1 pint)
Cider vinegar (1 quart)
White vinegar (1 quart)
Tarragon vinegar (1 pint)
Wine vinegar (1 pint)
Cornstarch or arrowroot flour (1 pound)
Granulated sugar (5 pounds)
Confectioners' sugar (1 pound)
Beef extract
Beef bouillon cubes
Chicken bouillon cubes
Worcestershire sauce
Imported curry powder
Chutney
Light brown sugar (1 pound)
Baker's German chocolate (1 pound)
Baker's unsweetened chocolate (1 pound)
Vanilla extract
Lemon extract
Almond extract
Unflavored gelatin
Seedless raisins

Long-grain rice
Minute rice
Vermicelli spaghetti
Macaroni
Canned home-style peaches
Canned pears
Bread crumbs
Tomato soup, condensed
Cream of mushroom soup, condensed
Dry mustard
Prepared mustard
Chicken and beef consommés which will jell
Several jars puréed fruit (baby food) for desserts
Tabasco (small bottle)
Garlic bud
Stick cinnamon
Powdered cinnamon
Whole cloves
Powdered cloves
Root ginger
Powdered ginger
Celery seed
Poultry seasoning
Barbecue sauce

In the refrigerator:
Parmesan cheese (in a piece; ¼ pound)
Blue cheese
Parsley
Pickled grated horseradish
Capers
Mayonnaise (1 pint)
Tomato paste (small can)
Pimiento (small can)
Lemons and other usual staples, such as milk, butter, etc.

In the freezer compartment:

Frozen raspberries
Frozen strawberries
Brown-and-serve rolls
Ice cream
Your favorite frozen vegetables or out-of-season frozen vege-
tables

HERB CHART

Basil: fish, tomato soup, eggs, liver, beef, tomatoes, spinach, peas, squash, onions, salads, tomato sauce

Bay leaf: boiled beef, poached fish, stews, pot roasts, tomatoes, gravies

Chervil: spinach, chicken or asparagus soup; eggs and
cheese, chicken, stuffings, steak, beets, celery, eggplant, carrots, salads, sauces made of poultry or fish
stock

Chives: potato and leek, bean or pea soup; eggs and cheese,
beef, pork, potatoes, peas, green salad, potato salad,
coleslaw, vinaigrette sauce

Dill: fish, eggs, cheese, veal, lamb, parsnips, potatoes, eggplant, beets, cucumber or potato salad, fish sauces

Marjoram: eggs, stuffings, stews, roasts, string beans, lima
beans, tomatoes, zucchini, spinach, peas, salads, gravies, fish sauces

Oregano: steak, roasts, stews, tomatoes, tomato soup

Rosemary: eggs, stuffings, veal, pork, lima beans, baked
beans, spinach

Sage: stuffings, fish chowders, pork, pork sausage, cabbage,
carrots, gravies

Savory: pea soup, lentil soup, eggs, cheese, stuffings, roast
veal, stews, peas, string beans, broccoli, cabbage,
carrots, beet or tomato salad, sauces made with
poultry or fish stock

Tarragon: tomato or chicken soup, eggs, fish, chicken, cabbage, tomatoes, peas, mushrooms, salads; tomato,
tartar and Béarnaise Sauce

Thyme: fish, stews, roasts, carrots, peas, onions, brown
sauces

Brunches, Lunches
and Suppers

Weekday breakfasts are apt to be rushed affairs these days, so I am going to give you recipes for late Sunday breakfasts or brunches — most of which, augmented by salad and dessert, would serve for lunch and several of which would do for a light supper. If, against his habit, your life's companion should suddenly demand eggs or French toast for breakfast on, say, Wednesday, you'll find directions here.

Before we start, there are a few little matters that had better be taken up. I'm sure that I don't have to tell you how to squeeze an orange, or that there are frozen concentrates, as well as fresh orange juice in cartons, on the market. There's a remote possibility, however, that you have never fixed a grapefruit. If you have the curved grapefruit knife it's easier, but it can be managed

with a straight knife. First cut the grapefruit in half crosswise, with the straight job. Take the curved one and cut
around the outside edge and between the sections. With
kitchen scissors, cut out the core. Sprinkle with sugar. To
select a grapefruit at the market, pick one that is heavy
and not discolored. It may be yellow or greenish but must
have no brown spots.

Melons, which you just cut in half or in sections and
seed, should be fragrant, have a hollow sound when you
knock them (you can sometimes hear the seeds rattle),
and be a little soft at the stem end. If you have made
friends with your fruit and vegetable man, which is a
good idea, trust him.

All I have to say about cooked cereal is to follow *exactly* the directions on the box. The cereal people have
finally realized that families are apt to be small at the
start, and they no longer direct you to make the whole
boxful. Instead, they now tell you how to make one or
two portions. So do what they say.

It is difficult for anyone to explain to someone else
exactly how to make good coffee. Tastes vary as does
equipment. You may like coffee strong, weak or medium;
you may have a percolator, a drip pot or a vacuum affair.
Buy the grind of coffee recommended for your type of
coffee maker and be sure that the latter is always ex-
quisitely clean. The standard amount of coffee to use is 2
level tablespoons per cup. Experiment with this and see
whether it is right for you. Experiment with brands of
coffee, too, and keep the kind you like in the tin or in a
canister, tightly covered. If you should find that no matter
what you do your coffee has a funny taste, it may be due

to the water. Instead of tap water, use bottled water or, if they are available in your vicinity, have a water filter installed. Incidentally, make your after-dinner coffee a little stronger than breakfast coffee. Most people prefer it that way no matter how they like it at other times.

Now, as to tea: unless you are married to an Englishman or are making tea for English people, tea bags are the answer. Of course if you are English yourself, you won't even be reading this; you'll know. So, if you must make real tea, I'll tell you how and save you from the ghastly thing that happened to a young friend of mine when she put tea leaves in a pot, added water and boiled and boiled. What a mess! What you must do is to rinse a china or earthenware teapot with hot water and, while the pot is still warm, put in it one teaspoon of tea leaves per cup. Pour in enough boiling water to cover the tea. Put the lid on the pot and let it stand, or steep, for 3 minutes. No more. Strain and add sufficient boiling water to make the tea the desired strength.

SCRAMBLED EGGS AND BACON

If you like very thin, crisp **bacon,** ask the butcher to slice it for you on No. 1. Otherwise, get packaged bacon, which is thicker but which you may prefer. Whatever kind you get, don't buy more than half a pound at a time for two people. The thin bacon must be taken out of the refrigerator at least half an hour before cooking or it will tear when you try to take it apart.

Take **4 or 5 eggs** out of the refrigerator. Eggs should always be at room temperature no matter what you're going to do with them.

Light the oven and put on top of it the plates you are going to use and a double thickness of paper toweling for draining the bacon.

Put your biggest iron skillet on the stove and heat it. If you want crisp, uncurled bacon, separate the strips and put them in the pan one by one. Lower the heat. With a fork, gently turn the bacon at intervals of a couple of minutes until the fat parts are no longer transparent. As each piece is done, lift it out and put it on the paper towel. This procedure will take about 15 minutes for ten strips of bacon. If you don't care about having the bacon flat, you don't need to separate the strips. Just put the amount you want into the skillet and pull it apart as it warms up. This takes a little less time than the other way, and if you like bacon slightly undercooked and soft, this is the way to go about it.

When the bacon is ready, pour the fat into a can; there is one especially for this purpose. It has a strainer on top, and if you put nothing in it except bacon grease, you have fine fat for cooking other things.

Break the eggs into a small bowl and add ¼ **teaspoon salt** and a **grinding of black pepper.** Stir the eggs with a fork.

Warn your husband that breakfast will be ready in no time. I'm taking it for granted that the coffee has been made or is making, fruit is on the table, and bread for toast is ready and waiting or rolls of some sort are in the oven.

In your smallest skillet, say a 6-incher, put **2 tablespoons of butter** and melt it over medium heat. (For lunch, you might add **a teaspoonful of chopped onion, parsley or ham** to the butter.) When the butter is bubbling, pour in the eggs. Leave them alone for a second while you put the bowl in which they were stirred into the sink and fill it with cold water. Go back to the eggs and stir them with the same fork, beginning with the outside edges, which are already beginning to get done. (This is the way you start an omelet, too.) Keep stirring until the eggs almost reach the consistency you like. Stop cooking, because they will firm up a little more on their way to the table. Put them on the plates and surround them with the bacon.

SCRAMBLED EGGS WITH SAUSAGES

There are several kinds of pork sausages, big and little, packaged and loose. Half a pound is sufficient for two, but if the brand you prefer comes only in 1-pound packages, buy the pound and plan a mixed grill for later in the week.

Three quarters of an hour before you cook the eggs, put the **sausages** in an iron skillet big enough so that they do not overlap. Add enough cold water to cover the bottom of the pan. Add a **pinch of sage.** Cover and simmer (boil gently) over medium heat for 5 minutes. Remove the lid and prick the sausages with a kitchen fork. After about 10 minutes, pour the water and grease down the drain in the kitchen sink. Have hot water running as you do this — it keeps the grease from clogging the drain. Hold the sausages in the skillet with the pancake turner. Return the pan to the stove and continue to cook over medium heat, turning the sausages often until they are brown. Start the **eggs** when the sausages are done. You can keep the latter warm on an asbestos pad over low heat. Sausages are also good with:

SHIRRED EGGS

Preheat the oven to 325°. **Butter,** rather lavishly, two individual shallow casseroles or shirred egg dishes. Break **2 eggs** carefully into each dish, sprinkle with **salt, a grinding of black pepper** and a **teaspoon of cream.** Dot with **1 tablespoon of butter.** The eggs will take from 12 to 18 minutes to bake, depending on how firm you want them; 18 minutes of cooking will produce quite hard eggs. So after the sausages have been on the fire for about a half hour, put the eggs in the oven. Look at them after 12 minutes and shake one of the dishes to see how firm the white is. Remove the eggs from the oven when they are done to your taste. They will keep hot.

For a luncheon dish, **cooked vegetables, minced ham** or **chicken (cooked),** or **bread crumbs** and **cheese** may be added. If you use any of these things, they should be put in the casserole before you put in the eggs.

BABY IN THE HOLE

This little arrangement can be served for breakfast with bacon or sausages or for a quick bite at noon, but it is most fun at a midnight snack, either for just the two of you or for a crowd.

With a 2½-inch cookie cutter, cut a hole out of the center of **one or more slices of bread.** In a frying pan big enough to hold the number of "babies" you're going to make, melt **2 tablespoons butter** for each slice of bread. Put the bread in the pan and cook, over low heat, until the underside of the bread just begins to brown. (Lift a corner of the bread with a spatula and peek.) Break **an egg** into each hole and sprinkle with **salt** and **pepper.**

When the whites of the eggs are set, turn the whole business with a pancake turner and cook for just a minute or two. Add more butter if the bread tends to stick. Lift out onto plates with the pancake turner. Some people might like a little tomato catsup on these eggs.

FRIED EGGS

Eggs may be fried in butter or bacon fat. They are more delicate if cooked in butter, but if you like the bacon flavor, leave enough bacon drippings in the skillet to make about **4 tablespoons of fat.** Otherwise, drain off the bacon fat (saving it in your storage can), wipe the skillet with paper towels, and add **4 tablespoons butter.** Heat until the fat is sizzling and break **4 eggs** into it. Reduce heat immediately and cook slowly for 3 to 4 minutes. Baste (spoon the fat over the eggs) as they cook. If you want the eggs sunny side up, you may cover the pan for the cooking period instead of basting. If you want them turned, use a pancake turner and cook for only a minute on the other side. Season with **salt** and **pepper** and lift out, onto warm plates, with the pancake turner.

OMELETS

There are two kinds of omelets, French and fluffy. Since you should not attempt to make an omelet with more than 5 eggs at the outside, a 10-inch skillet is the best size. If this is made of heavy aluminum or aluminum-lined copper, no treatment is needed before using it and no special care must be taken after using it. If your skillet is iron, it should be "seasoned." To do this, rub the new pan with steel wool. Put a tablespoon of peanut oil in it and clean it with paper towels. Fill with fresh oil (which can be put back in the bottle and used) and let it stand for 48 hours. Pour off the oil and wipe with paper towels. If possible, keep this skillet just for eggs, and after use, clean it by rubbing with salt and wiping with paper towels. It should never be really washed or scoured or allowed to soak in water, although I've found that a little, very hot water doesn't hurt it if used only occasionally. If you have to use the pan for other things, rinse it quickly with very hot water and scrub it with a clean brush. You can see that the other kind of pan is what you should have!

Omelets may be served with chicken livers, the recipe for which follows, or with Stewed Tomatoes.* Either of these accompaniments must be prepared before you start the omelet. The French omelet may have minced parsley and chives inside it, or your choice of finely chopped, cooked bacon, mushrooms, onions, potatoes, ham or chicken.

For the plain, French omelet, break **4 eggs** into a bowl. The eggs should be at room temperature, remember. Season them with **¼ teaspoon salt** and a **grinding of black pepper.**

Melt **¼ of a stick of butter** in the skillet over medium heat.

Stir the eggs with a fork until they are blended but not fluffy. When the butter sizzles, pour in the eggs and put the bowl to soak. Lower the heat and stir the eggs with the fork, from the outside in. Shake the pan. When the eggs are almost as firm as you'd like them for scrambled eggs, bang the pan on something handy like the top of the stove or the kitchen table and, with a spatula, fold half the mixture over onto the other half. Shake the pan

again. Turn off the heat and let the omelet sit in the pan
for a minute while you arrange the chicken livers, bacon
or what have you, on warm plates. Cut the omelet in half
and serve it quickly. Cooking time for this omelet is 3 to
4 minutes.

If you want **mushrooms** in the omelet, wash and dry
3 or 4. Cut off the tip of the stem (more if the mushrooms
are elderly and the stems are woody). About 15 minutes
before you start the omelet, put 1 tablespoon butter in
your smallest skillet and let it melt over medium heat.
Slice the mushrooms or chop them and put them in the
pan. Turn the heat to high and cook, uncovered, for 5
minutes. When the omelet is about ready to turn, take a
slotted spoon and scoop the mushrooms (no juice) into
the eggs. Put the pan to soak.

Onions should be chopped fine and sautéed (fried
lightly) in butter before being added, as the mushrooms
were, to the eggs. About 2 teaspoons of onions cooked in
1 teaspoon butter should be sufficient unless you are ab-
solutely mad for onions.

Chopped parsley and **chives** make an "omelette aux
fines herbes." Wash some of each and, with kitchen
shears, cut enough of each to make 1 tablespoon in all.
Add these to the eggs before they go into the pan.

Incidentally, if I'm confusing you by saying "chopped"
parsley and chives and then telling you to cut them, it is
because "chopped" is the word generally used for small
pieces of herbs. Actually, chives must always be cut; they
get mashed if you try to chop them. Parsley may be
chopped, but the flavor is better if it's cut. Have I made
myself clear?

Grated cheese, which I forgot to mention, may be added just before the omelet is turned. Other ingredients such as **cooked chicken, potatoes** or **ham** should be heated in a little butter before adding. They can be mixed with the eggs at the beginning, like the parsley and chives, or may be added when the omelet is about to be turned.

For the fluffy omelet, which many men seem to prefer, the eggs must be separated. I shall explain how to do this here and refer you to these instructions whenever the situation arises.

First of all, have the eggs at room temperature. In this case, you will need **4 eggs,** and also in this case, you must preheat the oven to 325° for the omelet. Have two bowls ready, one for the yolks and one for the whites. Crack an egg gently over the bowl in which the whites are going and, holding it upright, remove the top half of the shell, letting the white drip into the bowl. Carefully slide the yolk into the empty half shell, letting the white from the bottom half drip into the bowl. Tip the yolk from one half shell to the other until all the white is out. Drop the yolk into the other bowl. If any yolk gets into the whites, put the rest of the yolk in and begin over. Whites are good for nothing if any yolk gets into them. If you have had this accident, put the white and yolk in a small covered bowl, refrigerate it, and use it for scrambled eggs later on. By the same token, if you are using only the yolks, as in Hollandaise,* save the whites in the same manner.

Now the eggs have been separated. Add ¼ **teaspoon salt** to the whites and a **grinding of black pepper** to the yolks. Beat the yolks with a rotary beater until light in color. Rinse the beater with cold water and dry it. Then beat the whites with it or with a wire whisk until they are stiff and shiny and standing up in peaks.

Put a **generous tablespoon of butter** in the skillet and let it melt over moderate heat.

Pour the yolks over the whites and fold them in. This means to mix delicately with a down, up and over motion. When the butter sizzles, pour the omelet mixture into the pan. Level the surface gently with a spatula. Reduce the heat and cook slowly for 5 minutes. Lift the omelet at the edge with the spatula and see whether the bottom is lightly browned. When it is, put the skillet in the oven and bake the omelet from 12 to 15 minutes, until a silver knife, inserted at the center, comes out clean. To serve, tear in half gently, using two forks. Invert halves on warm plates so that the browned bottom becomes the top.

CHICKEN LIVERS AND MUSHROOMS

These are good served on buttered toast, on rice,* with Scrambled Eggs* or with an Omelet.* Later on, I'm going to tell you how to make giblet gravy for roast chicken, but, in the event that neither of you care for gravy, save the livers for this recipe. You will find them, along with other items such as the gizzard and heart, in a small package inside the chicken (or duck or turkey). Wash them, wrap them in freezer paper and freeze them.

☞ **HAVE ON HAND**
> **6 fresh chicken livers or an equal amount of frozen livers**
> **3 or 4 mushrooms**

onion
butter
flour
chicken bouillon cube
bay leaf, thyme
salt, pepper
Madeira (optional)
parsley

Melt 2 tablespoons butter in a medium-sized skillet over moderate heat. Add 1 teaspoon minced onion and 1 teaspoon chopped (cut) parsley. Lower heat and allow to cook gently.

Wash and dry 3 or 4 mushrooms, cut off the bottom of the stems, and slice into the butter.

If the chicken livers are fresh, wash them and pat them dry with paper towels. If they are frozen, thaw them and dry them. Cut them in small pieces with kitchen shears and add them. Cook, stirring, for 3 or 4 minutes.

Sprinkle the livers with 1 tablespoon flour and cook, stirring occasionally, until flour browns.

Have ready ¾ cup broth made by dissolving 1 chicken bouillon cube in ¾ cup boiling water. Pour this into the livers. Add 1 small bay leaf and a pinch of thyme, salt and pepper to taste. Simmer, uncovered, for 20 minutes. If you're having this for luncheon or supper, add a scant tablespoon Madeira. The whole business takes about a half hour, as you can see, but the livers can wait, on an asbestos pad over low heat. They can also be frozen and heated when needed.

POACHED EGGS

This is not the easiest way to cook eggs, but with practice it can be conquered. If you want to be a sissy, there are egg poachers on the market.

Have **4 very fresh eggs** at room temperature. Have 2 inches of water boiling in a shallow pan. Add **1 teaspoon white or cider vinegar** to the water. Reduce the heat until the water is steadily simmering — just barely bubbling. Break each egg into a cup and slide it into the water. Cover the pan, turn off the heat, and let stand 5 minutes. The eggs can be removed from the water now, with a slotted spoon, put on buttered toast, and served, sprinkled with salt and pepper. Or they may be slipped into a bowl filled with warm salted water, where they can wait, if necessary.

EGGS BENEDICT

☞ **HAVE ON HAND**

6 eggs	English muffins
lemon	2 thin slices raw ham
butter	salt, pepper

Since Hollandaise Sauce can wait, make it first, as follows:

Have 2 eggs and ½ lemon at room temperature. Allow ¼ pound butter to soften.

Separate the eggs, dropping the yolks into a small earthenware or iron casserole (preferably one with a handle). Put the whites in a tightly covered small bowl and refrigerate for later use. Add the strained juice of the half lemon to the yolks and sprinkle with salt and freshly ground black pepper.

Divide the butter into three parts. Put the casserole on an asbestos pad over low heat. Stir with a wooden spoon and add 1 piece of butter. Continue to stir, and when the butter has melted, add the second piece. Repeat the process with the third piece. Cook and stir until thick. This won't take long. Put the casserole on the back of the stove in a warm but not hot place. It can wait happily for 15 to 20 minutes. Stir again before using.

If you have an electric blender, there are instructions for making Hollandaise in the booklet that came with it. My way is really easiest, though.

Preheat the oven to 350°. Split 2 large English muffins with a fork. Butter each half.

Cut each slice of ham in two and trim the pieces so that they are a little larger than the muffins. They shrink a bit as they cook. Put 1 teaspoon butter in a skillet and melt over moderate heat. Add the slices of ham.

Put the muffins on a cookie sheet and set them under the broiler. Watch carefully so that they don't burn. When they are golden brown turn off the oven. They will wait until you are ready for them.

Turn the ham. Poach 4 eggs.* Put the muffins on warm plates. Put the ham on the muffins, the eggs on the ham and pour the sauce over all. Better allow a good three quarters of an hour to get this brunch into condition.

BOILED EGGS

There is a little electric gadget for boiling eggs or, to be accurate, for steaming them. You put in the amount of water indicated for 2-, 3-, 4-minute, or hard-boiled eggs, set the eggs in their holders, put the top on, and plug the thing in. When the eggs are ready, it turns off with a loud snap that invariably makes me drop whatever it is that I have in my hand.

Lacking the gadget, the best boiled **eggs**, whether soft or hard-cooked, are made by the cold-water method, which is called coddling. You put them (they are at room temperature, of course) into a pan of cold water, enough to cover them, add a **pinch of salt,** and turn on the heat. The salt keeps the eggs from running if they should crack. Watch the pan out of the corner of your eye while you do other things. When the water reaches a boil, turn the heat down so that it merely simmers and start timing: 1 minute for a 2-minute egg, 1½ minutes for a 3-minute egg, 2 minutes for a 4-minute egg, and 15 minutes for a hard-boiled egg. The whites cook slowly by this method and never get rubbery. When hard-boiled eggs are done, plunge them immediately into cold water and let them get quite cool before refrigerating them. This keeps the yolks from turning green.

WAFFLES AND PANCAKES

As you undoubtedly know, there are frozen waffles and pancakes on the market as well as mixes which may be used for either. The latter may be enriched by the addition of an egg or melted shortening, but they are quite good as they are. If you have been given a waffle iron as a wedding present, you might like to impress *him* — or the donor — by making your own waffles from scratch. Here is a simple recipe which is both foolproof and double-barreled. It is foolproof, that is, if you follow the directions that came with your waffle iron. It is double-barreled because you can also make pancakes out of it.

Sift 1½ cups all-purpose flour with 2 teaspoons baking powder, 2 teaspoons sugar and ½ teaspoon salt.

Beat 2 eggs with a rotary beater and add to them 1 cup milk and ¼ cup peanut oil or melted butter. Stir into the flour. Don't bother about some lumps. Bake the waffles as directed. (If you are serving them with creamed chicken, omit the sugar.)

For pancakes, thin the batter with enough milk to make it the consistency of light cream. Heat a griddle or an iron skillet. Spill a drop of water on it and if it sizzles and forms a ball, turn down heat a touch so that the griddle or skillet will hold that temperature and drop spoonfuls of batter on or into it. Use no grease. As soon as bubbles form, turn the pancakes. Turn only once. Lift them out and keep them warm in stacks in the oven. Again, if you are serving the pancakes as an entrée or with caviar, omit the sugar. The size of the cakes depends on the amount of batter you use for each one. They may be made with a teaspoonful of batter, a tablespoonful or even more.

The batter will last for three days in the refrigerator.

FRENCH TOAST

Trim the crust or not, as you prefer, from **4 to 6 slices of two-day-old bread.**

Beat **2 eggs** lightly, with a fork, and stir in **1 cup milk, ¼ teaspoon salt** and **1 teaspoon sugar.** A grating of **nutmeg** may be added. Pour the mixture into a shallow dish large enough to hold the bread. Put the bread to soak. Turn the pieces once.

Melt **½ stick of butter** in a large skillet, and when it is bubbling, add as many slices of egg-soaked bread as will fit in. Lower the heat to medium. In a minute or two, lift a corner of a slice with a spatula and peek. When the underside is brown, turn it and brown the other side. As each piece of toast is done, remove it and put it in a warm oven on a cookie sheet covered with paper toweling. French toast may be served with syrup, jam, honey, fruit, or with brown sugar and sour cream. The latter combination is my invention.

CREAMED CHIPPED BEEF

Open a **package of chipped beef** and tear the pieces apart. Put them in a bowl and cover with warm water. Let them stand for a few minutes and drain.

In a saucepan, melt **2 tablespoons butter** over moderate heat. Add the chipped beef and sauté for 3 minutes. Sprinkle with **1 tablespoon flour** and stir until blended. Add **1½ cups milk, cream,** or **half-and-half** (half milk, half cream). Simmer until thick. Season with freshly **ground black pepper** and add **1 tablespoon Madeira.** Serve on **baked potatoes*** or on **buttered toast.**

LAMB KIDNEYS

No English breakfast would be complete without grilled
lamb kidneys to accompany the scrambled eggs. They
are split, brushed with melted butter, broiled very quickly
under high heat, and seasoned with salt and pepper.
Here is a luncheon or supper dish that's a happy combination of kidneys and noodles.

☞ **HAVE ON HAND**

6 lamb kidneys	small white onions
flour	beef bouillon cube
butter	2 eggs
salt, black peppercorns	8-ounce package noodles

Wash the kidneys and slice them thin. Put them in a
paper bag with ½ cup flour, ¼ teaspoon salt and a grinding of black pepper. Shake the bag, coating the kidneys
with the seasoned flour. Mince 2 small white onions. Put
1 quart water on to boil in a deep saucepan. Put 1 teaspoon salt in it.

Melt 1½ tablespoons butter in a medium-sized skillet
over high heat. Add the kidneys and cook quickly, stirring
with a fork. As soon as the kidneys are brown, add the
minced onions and reduce the heat. Dissolve ½ bouillon
cube in ¾ cup boiling water and add. Simmer for 10
minutes.

The water for the noodles should be boiling now, so
put in ½ package. Cook for 9 to 12 minutes, until soft.
Drain and put into a colander over hot water.

Now you are going to "bind" a sauce with egg yolks.
This is the most delicate way of thickening a sauce. Separate 2 eggs.* Save the whites as described elsewhere. Beat

the yolks until thick, with a rotary beater. Take a spoonful of sauce from the kidneys and stir it into the egg yolks. Add this mixture to the kidneys. Stir, over low heat, for just a few seconds until the sauce is fairly thick. Turn off the heat.

Put the noodles in a warm serving dish and toss them with 1 tablespoon butter. Empty the kidney skillet over the noodles and serve.

CHEESE SOUFFLÉ

Breakfasts having been taken care of, we're cooking for lunch now or, in this case, possibly for supper. Don't let the idea of a soufflé scare you. All you need to turn out a beauty is a good oven that will hold its heat, a 1-quart soufflé dish, a wire whisk, the ingredients and a will. This soufflé takes about an hour, but for 35 minutes of that time, it is on its own in the oven.

☞ HAVE ON HAND

milk	cayenne pepper
butter	Parmesan cheese (¼-pound piece)
flour	2 eggs
salt	

Preheat the oven to 350°. Grate enough cheese to make ¼ cup. Put ½ cup milk in a saucepan or measuring cup on an asbestos pad over moderate heat. The milk should get hot, but it shouldn't boil. When bubbles form, turn off the heat. The milk is "scalded."

Melt 4 tablespoons butter in a heavy saucepan over moderate heat. With a wooden spoon, stir in 2 tablespoons flour. This is called making a "roux." Add the hot milk gradually and stir until the sauce is thick and smooth. Add ½ teaspoon salt, a dash of cayenne pepper and the grated cheese. Stir until the cheese has melted and turn off the heat.

Separate the eggs.* Beat the yolks with a rotary beater until they are light in color. Add a little of the hot sauce to the yolks and stir. Add a little more, stirring, and then add the lot. Cover the bowl and put it in the refrigerator while you beat the egg whites.

If you have an electric mixer with a wire whisk attachment, use it. Beat the whites until they are stiff but not dry; they must stand up in glistening peaks. Lacking an electric mixer of this type, put the whites in a large bowl and start the beating with a rotary beater. As soon as the whites are frothy, switch to a wire whisk. The whisk gets more air into the whites, and, as you will see, when they reach the glistening peak stage, there will be no liquid in the bottom of the bowl. In fact, you can turn the bowl upside down and the whites will stay put. If you have the energy to use the wire whisk from the start, so much the better. Incidentally, whenever you are making a soufflé, use an extra egg white or two if you have some around which aren't more than two or three days old.

Take the sauce from the refrigerator. It should be fairly cool by this time. Stir about ⅓ of the whites into it. Just stir as if you were adding milk or water. Then pour the sauce over the rest of the whites and fold in ever so gently — and briefly. It doesn't matter if there are spots of egg white showing. Pour the mixture into an unbuttered, 1-quart soufflé dish, pop it into the oven, and forget it for 35 minutes. Don't worry or peek. It will be beautiful. Just be on hand to eat it as soon as it's ready.

If you use extra egg whites in any soufflé, it's a good idea to put a collar of waxed paper around the dish to keep the soufflé from rising too far and spilling over. To do this, tear off a piece of waxed paper long enough to encircle the dish and overlap slightly. Fold it in half lengthwise and wrap it around the dish so that it sticks up a good 2 inches above the top. Fasten it with scotch tape or paper clips.

The cheese sauce may be made long ahead of time, combined with the egg yolks, and left to wait, covered, until you are ready to beat the whites and cook the soufflé.

CHEESE MONKEY

This is a sort of a fake cheese soufflé. If you haven't the nerve or the proper equipment to make the McCoy, try this. It is simple to make but good enough to serve to guests at an informal luncheon or supper party. Lettuce and tomato salad and a dessert might complete the meal. This recipe is for *four*.

Cut the crusts from **8 slices white bread.** Butter a baking dish that will hold 4 of them. You can cut the slices to fit if necessary. Put the 4 slices in the dish and cover them with **¼ pound American or rat-trap cheese,** sliced thin. Cover with the other 4 slices of bread. Beat **3 eggs** lightly, with a fork, and combine them with **2 cups milk, ½ teaspoon salt,** a **grinding of black pepper** and a **pinch of powdered sage.** Pour this into the baking dish and put in the refrigerator for an hour or longer — longer if possible.

Preheat the oven to 350°. Remove the baking dish from

the refrigerator about 15 minutes before putting it in the oven. Then bake for 35 minutes.

WELSH RAREBIT

Melt **1 tablespoon butter** in a saucepan and blend in **1 teaspoon cornstarch.** Add **½ cup milk or beer** and bring to the boiling point, stirring constantly. Add **1½ cups diced, unprocessed American cheese** and stir over low heat until the cheese has melted. Add **½ teaspoon dry mustard, 1 teaspoon Worcestershire sauce, a dash of cayenne pepper** and **salt** to taste. Serve on hot buttered toast or rusks. Beer is good with this.

FONDUE NEUFCHÂTELOISE

This is fun to serve to guests, but it's just as much fun for two. You will need a chafing dish or an earthenware casserole with a handle and an electric plate to put it on. Of course, for just the two of you, you can rough it in the kitchen and put the casserole on the stove.

☞ **HAVE ON HAND**
      ½ **pound imported Swiss cheese**
      flour
      garlic (optional)
      dry white wine
      salt, black peppercorns, nutmeg
      kirschwasser, applejack, Cognac or light rum
      French bread or 4 hard rolls

Shred the cheese and put it in a paper bag with 1 cup flour. Shake the bag. This is called "dredging" the cheese with flour.

Rub the cooking utensil with garlic (or don't) and put

in it 1 cup dry white wine. If you're using a chafing dish, put the pan directly over a very low fire; if you're using a casserole, put it on an asbestos pad on the electric plate or over low heat on the stove. When the wine is heated just to the point when bubbles rise to the surface but is *not* boiling, stir with a fork while you add handfuls of cheese, letting each handful dissolve before adding the next. Keep stirring until the mixture starts bubbling. Add a pinch of salt and a grinding of black pepper and nutmeg. Add 3 tablespoons kirschwasser or 2 tablespoons applejack, Cognac or light rum. Keep the fondue hot and bubbling. If it gets too thick, thin it with a little heated wine.

Cut the French bread or the rolls into bite-sized pieces. Each of you alternately spears a piece of bread with a fork, going through the soft part and securing the prongs in the crust. Now dunk the bread in the fondue, one at a time. Use a stirring motion which both maintains the consistency of the fondue and assures that each piece of bread is thoroughly coated with cheese. Towards the end of this feast, some of the melted cheese will form a brown crust at the bottom of the utensil. When that happens, lift it out with a fork and share it or fight for it. It is delicious.

Appetizers and Soups

APPETIZERS

I doubt that you will go in for appetizers to any great extent until you are ready for serious entertaining. However, you will probably have occasion to serve cocktails to a small group before you all go out to dinner, so here are a few tidbits that you could whip up for staving off hunger pangs.

CRISPED CHIPPED BEEF

Try to find the **chipped beef** that comes in squares. Pull it apart gently and spread the squares on a cookie sheet. Melt **½ stick unsalted butter** (this is important because the chipped beef is salty) and, using a pastry brush, dab the butter all over each square. Turn on the oven to 250°. Put the cookie sheet under the broiler about 2 inches from the heating element. Watch carefully to see that the beef doesn't burn. After about 10 minutes, take the pan out and put the dark red and shriveled, but delicious, squares on paper toweling in a pie plate. Keep them warm and make more. They crisp up when they are out of the oven but they shouldn't be kept waiting too long. Eat them like potato chips. Another thing to eat like potato chips:

BAKED POTATO SKINS

Bake **3 or 4 Idaho potatoes.*** Scoop them out. Save the insides for mashed potatoes or potato cakes. Cut the skins into strips or squares and brush with **melted butter.** Sprinkle with **paprika** and toast in a medium oven (350°) until crisp. People love these.

CREAM CHEESE PUFFS

Beat **1 egg** and mix it with **1 small package cream cheese** until the mixture has the consistency of a thick paste. Add the egg little by little, but don't use all of it; that would make it too liquid. Add **1 teaspoon grated onion** and **salt** to taste.

Preheat the oven to 375°.

With a small cookie cutter, cut about a dozen rounds out of **sandwich bread.** Put these on a cookie sheet and toast under the broiler on one side only. Spread the other side with the cheese and pop back into the oven until brown and puffy.

SHRIMP IN BEER

Your beau will like these; in fact he might even like to help make them. They are shelled before cooking, which not only makes them more delicate but keeps the whole house from smelling of fish. This recipe will make enough shrimp for 6 to 8 people, depending on how hungry they are. Cook them early in the day so that they may be chilled.

☞**HAVE ON HAND**

3 pounds raw shrimp
2 cans or bottles of beer
dry mustard
celery seed (or celery leaves)
 mayonnaise

cayenne pepper
white vinegar
garlic (optional)
salt

Wash the shrimp. If you have the Shrimpmaster, the whole operation of peeling and deveining is done with one motion. Directions come with the gadget. If you don't have this, peel off the shell with your fingers and take out the black vein with the point of a beer can opener or with a toothpick.

Combine in a deep saucepan the beer, 1 clove garlic crushed with 1 tablespoon salt (if you don't like garlic, just add the salt), 2 tablespoons dry mustard, 4 tablespoons celery seed or a bunch of celery leaves, ½ teaspoon cayenne pepper and ¼ cup white vinegar. Bring to a boil, add the shrimp, and cook 5 minutes — until the shrimp are pink. Cool in broth. Drain and chill.

These shrimp are so flavorful that it is a pity to serve cocktail sauce with them. Plain mayonnaise is best.

PLAIN BOILED SHRIMP

Wash the shrimp; peel and devein them as above. Bring to a boil enough water to cover them. Add 1 tablespoon salt for 3 pounds of shrimp. Add shrimp and cook 5 minutes. Cool in broth. Drain, chill and serve this special sauce: mix together **1 cup mayonnaise, ½ cup tomato catsup, 1½ teaspoons Worcestershire sauce, 1 teaspoon** dry mustard, 1½ tablespoons chopped chives and ½ cup dry sherry. Chill.

SOUPS

Believe it or not, the most important item in soup making in today's kitchens, and especially in yours, is the can opener. Few of us can make soup as well as a good manufacturer. We have neither the time, the equipment or the know-how. Time-honored and time-consuming recipes created by master chefs are followed to the letter in the kitchens of good manufacturers. The trick of being creative about soup, while not actually making it, lies in the imaginative use of added seasonings and in combining different canned soups. Your herb chart will give you ideas about seasoning, such as adding basil or oregano to tomato soup, chives to pea soup, tarragon to chicken soup, and so forth.

As for combining soups, the sky is the limit. As a matter of fact a man wrote a book about how to make 480 different soups out of 5 cans. We don't need to go into all that. I will give you several classic combinations, and you can take it from there and experiment.

Consommé Bellevue: half clear chicken consommé and half clam broth with or without a dollop of whipped cream.

Boula: half green turtle soup and half pea soup with 1 teaspoon Madeira added at the last minute, and a float of whipped cream.

Oyster Soup Louisianne: half cream of oyster soup and half cream of tomato soup.

Purée Mongole: equal parts of condensed tomato soup, condensed pea soup, and water, garnished with croutons.

Wines may also be used, in very small quantities, to add flavor to canned soups; a teaspoon of sherry complements beef consommé, chicken soup or turtle soup; a teaspoon of Madeira does the same for vegetable soup, as does the same amount of dry white wine or vermouth in fish chowders. Always add wine at the last minute so that the delicate flavor will not be cooked away.

Besides canned soups there are frozen soups, concentrates and dehydrated soups. Try them and see which you like. The dehydrated variety take up very little space on the emergency shelf. Have soup; it's good and it's good for you. Have a thick soup before a light meal and a bouillon before a heavy meal and don't forget that there are consommés which jell when refrigerated. Incidentally, don't chill one of these for the drink known as a "bull shot" (vodka, cold beef bouillon and seasonings). You'd have to eat it with a spoon!

Meat

HOW TO SHOP FOR MEAT

First of all, tame your butcher. You can charm him, in the beginning, with the helpless young bride approach, but this can't go on forever. Its effectiveness is diminished by use. Besides, some butchers may take advantage of your ignorance and foist inferior cuts or low-grade meat upon you. It's much better to know your onions, so to speak, before you beard the butcher in his den. Win his respect. To do this, read what I have to say about meat, as a starter, and study what other books have to say about it. Go to the butcher armed with specific knowledge of what you want. You must be able to tell whether the pork chops he is cutting are center cut, which you asked for, or not. Some of this knowledge must come, of course, from experience. You can learn a lot during the helpless young bride stage by watching other people buy. I am going to give you all the help I can right now.

Beef, veal and lamb are graded by government inspectors, and the round stamp, which guarantees whole-some meat, is put on the retail cuts with harmless purple ink, as is the stamp of quality. There are three grades of meat: Prime, Choice and Good. Prime meat is grabbed up by hotels and restaurants. If you can find it and afford it, it is the best. Choice is almost as good, however, and that is what we all usually buy. Meat stamped "Good" needs long, slow cooking but is perfectly acceptable for stew and pot roasts.

The best beef is firm, finely grained and has a marbling or intermingling of fat with the lean. The fat on the out-side is firm, brittle, and somewhat waxy. Aged beef, while it does not look as pretty as bright red unaged beef, is in-finitely superior in taste and tenderness. If you buy pack-aged beef, buy the packages which are marked "aged" unless the budget is in dire straits. Beef is good all year round.

Veal is at its best in spring and early summer. It has no marbling of fat. It should be velvety in appearance and light pink in color. The paler pink the meat, the younger and tenderer the veal. The outside fat should be clear, firm, and white.

Good-quality lamb, which is best in summer and fall, has clear, white, brittle fat, and the lean is pinkish-red in color. The older the lamb, the darker red the meat. Lamb has a thin paperlike covering over the outside of the whole carcass which is known as the fell. This is left on a leg of lamb during cooking, since it does not affect the flavor, keeps the leg of lamb in shape, allows it to cook in less time, and keeps it juicier. Chops, however, should have the fell removed before cooking. If the butcher doesn't do it, and occasionally he doesn't, you do it. You will probably be removing some of the fat anyway.

The fat of pork, which is cold-weather meat, indicates its quality. It should be firm and white. The color of the lean of young pork is grayish-pink, turning to a delicate rose in older pork. It is well marbled, and the texture is firm.

Since all four-legged animals are similar in shape, the cuts from them are the same in contour; they simply vary in size. The cuts which you will be most apt to buy are as follows:

An oval shape with a round bone in the widest part is, in beef, the round steak. This may be ground for hamburger, cut in cubes for stews, or braised. In veal, it is the cutlet, which may be cut thin for scallopini or for breaded cutlets. In pork, you will find it as either a center-cut pork chop or a smoked ham slice. In lamb, it is a lamb steak.

A slice of meat which has two straight sides and one curving side with an oval-shaped bone is, in beef, the sirloin steak. You will not be apt to use this cut in other meats.

A piece of meat with a bone shaped like a T can be three things in beef. At its largest, it is the porterhouse steak, the next size is the T-bone steak, and the smallest is the club steak. All these are excellent steaks. When the fillet, or small section of one side of the bone is removed, you have a strip steak. In veal, this cut is a loin chop, as it is also in lamb and pork. These are fine chops.

When a rib bone curves along one side of the meat and turns the corner, you have, in beef, a rib steak; and in veal, lamb and pork, you have rib chops.

➳✳❧☯✳❧☯✳❧☯✳❧☯✳❧☯✳❧☯✳❧☯✳❧☯✳❧☯✳❧☯✳❧☯✳❧☯✳

I'm sure that you know what a standing rib roast of beef looks like and what spareribs look like (always buy meaty ones), so we needn't go into that. You'll also recognize a leg of lamb or veal. The cuts I've described seem to be the most important for you to know about at the start. Trust your butcher about such things as rump or chuck pot roasts, breasts of lamb or veal, and those delicacies known as variety meats. The latter are calves' liver, veal and lamb kidneys, heart, tongue, sweetbreads, and brains. Don't overlook them. They are wonderful eating and full of vitamins and minerals. Tongue is usually smoked, but all the rest are fresh and perishable. You should not shop for them more than a day in advance.

If you want to freeze fresh meat such as steaks or chops, be sure to wrap it snugly in aluminum foil or freezer paper so that no air gets into it. Label the package as to contents and date of purchase.

BROILED LAMB CHOPS; MINT JELLY
PEAS WITH MUSHROOMS*
BAKED POTATOES
ICE CREAM

Here is a simple little dinner for your first evening at home. I suggest ice cream for dessert because it's easy and men like it, but you can use your own judgment. If you'd like to make a dessert earlier in the day, there are lots of easy ones in the dessert section. Also, if you'd rather have the peas plain, don't buy the mushrooms or cream.

❋ᵛ☙❋ᵛ☙❋ᵛ☙❋ᵛ☙❋ᵛ☙❋ᵛ☙❋ᵛ☙❋ᵛ☙❋ᵛ☙❋ᵛ☙❋ᵛ

Instructions for peas both ways are in the vegetable section.

☞ **HAVE ON HAND**

    2 double loin or rib lamb chops (ask for chops with a wide "eye")
    garlic bud (unless you don't like a touch of garlic)
    1 glass mint jelly
    2 Idaho potatoes
    1 pound fresh peas or 1 package frozen peas
    ¼ pound mushrooms
    ½ pint cream
    butter, flour
    nutmeg
    Lawry's Seasoned Salt
    black peppercorns
    salt, paprika

One hour before dinner, take the chops out of the refrigerator. If you are broiling the chops in the stove, turn on the oven to 400° at the same time. (If you are using an electric broiler, this is not necessary. Preheat it if and when the booklet that came with it says to.) Pull 1 clove of garlic out of the garlic bud, skin it with a knife, cut it in half, and rub it over the chops. Rub them also with Lawry's Salt and freshly ground black pepper. Make several cuts in the fat sides.

Scrub the potatoes and rub them with butter. Put them in the oven and test them with a kitchen fork in 40 minutes. If they are soft, take them out, cut a gash in them to let the steam escape, put a lump of butter in each, and keep them warm on top of the stove.

While the potatoes are baking, shell the peas, if you are having them. Cook the peas* by either recipe and

✦✳✦✳✦✳✦✳✦✳✦✳✦✳✦✳✦✳✦✳✦✳✦✳✦✳✦✳✦✳✦✳✦

keep them warm in an ovenproof dish or casserole on an asbestos pad over very low heat.

Half an hour before dinner, put the chops on the broiler rack and put the rack into position so that the top of the meat is 1½ to 2 inches from the heat. Prop the broiler door slightly ajar if you are cooking with gas; if your stove is electric, leave it wide open. Brown (sear) the chops on one side, turn them, and sear the other side. Lower the heat to 350° and if your chops are 2 inches thick, cook them for 20 minutes from the time you put them in. If they are less than 2 inches thick, 18 minutes will be sufficient. When the cooking time is up, turn off the oven and let the chops rest.

You now have 10 minutes for last-minute things. Add a little more butter with some salt and pepper or paprika to the potatoes and mash them, inside, with a fork. Fix the salad, if you're having it. Put the mint jelly in a dish. Dinner plates, I hope, are heating on top of the stove, and rolls have been heated or browned before the oven was turned off. Dinner should be ready.

MIXED GRILL
GREEN SALAD*
CHOCOLATE MOUSSE*

If you have had pork sausages for Sunday brunch and have half a pound left over, plan this menu for Tuesday night. One nice thing about this dinner, everything goes on one plate; one plate each, that is, and hot. Make the

*〜☙〜✻〜☙〜✻〜☙〜✻〜☙〜✻〜☙〜✻〜☙〜✻〜☙〜✻〜☙〜✻〜☙〜✻〜☙〜✻〜

Chocolate Mousse* the day before or make some other
dessert early in the day.

☞ HAVE ON HAND
> 2 double loin lamb chops with or without kidneys in
> them
> ½ pound pork sausages
> 1 large Bermuda onion
> 1 large tomato
> 4 large mushrooms
> Lawry's Seasoned Salt
> black peppercorns, salt
> garlic (optional)
> butter
> rosemary

One hour before dinner, take the chops and sausages
out of the refrigerator. Treat the chops as in the previous
recipe and light the oven, turning it to 400°. If you would
like baked potatoes with this dinner, fix them as just
described.

Peel the onion, holding it under running cold water.
Put it in a saucepan and cover it with water. This is to see
how much water you will need to cover it. Remove the
onion and put the water on to boil with a pinch of salt.
When it is boiling, put in the onion and cook it until
barely tender — about 15 minutes. Drain and cool it and
cut it into ½-inch-thick slices.

Wash the tomato, slice off the stem end, and cut it in
half. Sprinkle with Lawry's Salt, freshly ground black pepper and a pinch of rosemary.

Put the sausages* on to cook.

Put ½ stick butter in a small saucepan over low heat to
melt.

Wash the mushrooms but do not peel them. Cut off the stems flush with the bottoms.

Half an hour before dinner, start the chops as in the previous recipe. When the heat has been lowered, arrange the onion slices, the tomato halves and the mushrooms on the rack beside the chops. Brush them with melted butter, using the pastry brush. Turn them when they are slightly brown and brush again with butter. They will be ready when the chops are, as will the sausages. Later on, when you have conquered sweetbreads,* a pair may be added to the group under the broiler. They should be parboiled,* of course, and brushed with melted butter along with the rest of the mixed grill.

Once again I am taking it for granted that the rolls have been coped with, that the salad greens were washed earlier, and that now everything is ready.

BROILED STEAK
ASPARAGUS WITH BROWNED BUTTER
HASH BROWNED POTATOES*
APPLE PIE

This is in the nature of a celebratory dinner; it will not be much trouble, but it won't be cheap. A good steak never is. So why not go all out and make it a party? Have Apple Pie.* You can take care of that early in the day.

☞ **HAVE ON HAND**
    1 porterhouse steak or 2 strip sirloin steaks cut 1¼
        inches thick
    garlic (optional)
    1 package frozen asparagus or 1 pound fresh asparagus
    butter
    2 large Irish potatoes
    onion
    salt, peppercorns
    lemon
    thyme, marjoram, rosemary
    Lawry's Seasoned Salt

While your pie is baking, wash the potatoes, put enough water in a saucepan to cover them, and when it is boiling, put the potatoes in with a teaspoon of salt. When they are tender, in a half hour or so, drain and cool them.

One hour before dinner, take the steak or steaks out of the refrigerator. Turn on the oven to 400°. Treat the meat as you do lamb chops,* cutting slashes in the fat, rubbing it with garlic, Lawry's Salt and pepper. Then rub in pinches of thyme, marjoram and rosemary.

Look up the recipe for Hashed Browned Potatoes* and prepare them.

If you are having fresh asparagus,* get it ready for cooking.

Your steak will take between 15 and 25 minutes to cook, depending on how thick it is and how well-done you like it. The cooking procedure is the same as for lamb chops. Time it, and other kinds of steak, according to the table at the end of this recipe, being sure to let it rest at least 10 minutes before carving.

While the steak is cooking, do the asparagus. While

the asparagus is cooking, put ½ stick butter in a small skillet and let it get golden brown over medium heat. Watch so that it doesn't burn. When it is ready put an asbestos pad under it, and turn down the heat.

When the asparagus is done, drain it thoroughly and keep it warm over hot water. When ready to serve, place it on a hot plate or plates and pour the butter over it.

Cut 2 slices of lemon and put a small dab of butter on each. These go on top of each portion of steak; very good, as you'll see.

Porterhouse	**Rare**	**Medium**
1 inch thick	15 minutes	20 minutes
1½ inches thick	20 minutes	25 minutes
2 inches thick	25 minutes	30 minutes
Rib Steak		
1 inch thick	15 minutes	20 minutes
1½ inches thick	20 minutes	25 minutes
2 inches thick	25 minutes	30 minutes
Club or Strip		
1 inch thick	12 minutes	15 minutes
1½ inch thick	18 minutes	20 minutes
2 inches thick	20 minutes	25 minutes
Filet Mignon		
1 inch thick	12 minutes	15 minutes
1½ inches thick	15 minutes	20 minutes

Note: To broil steaks in an electric broiler, follow directions for that particular broiler.

Note 2: If you have an electric stove, leave the oven door open while broiling. With a gas stove, leave it ajar.

❀↝❀✳❀↝❀✳❀↝❀✳❀↝❀✳❀↝❀✳❀↝❀✳❀↝❀✳❀↝❀✳❀↝❀✳❀↝❀✳

ROAST BEEF
CAULIFLOWER AU GRATIN*
BROWNED POTATOES AND ONIONS
PEACHES OR PEARS, RASPBERRY SAUCE*

The larger the roast, the better it tastes. It is not extravagant to get a 7-pound standing rib roast. You will get three meals and some sandwiches out of it and you won't be bored. The way to go about this is to half cook, or "set," the roast for the first meal. Have two nice slices apiece from each side, one outside cut and one pink piece. Refrigerate but do not freeze the rest of the roast. Two days later, put the roast in the oven again, dusting the cut sides with fresh seasoning, and complete the cooking. Have a different vegetable, potatoes another way (Hashed Browned Potatoes* perhaps, especially if you have, with malice aforethought, cooked extra potatoes the first time) and something else for dessert. After that dinner, make Miroton of Beef* and freeze it for some evening when you want to prepare dinner in a hurry.

There are two methods of roasting beef: searing and not searing. To sear means to put the meat in a 500° oven for 20 minutes and then reduce the heat for the rest of the cooking time. This method insures a crispy brown outside. The nonsearing method cuts down shrinkage and cooking losses, or drippings. It takes a little longer, since the oven temperature stays at 325°. Whichever method you follow, if you cook the roast completely the first time, which you might do if you are having company, it will take approximately 2 hours; if you set it, it will take 1 hour, so plan accordingly, remembering to allow time for it to rest for 10 to 15 minutes when it is done.

Since the cauliflower* must cook in a 450° oven for 15 minutes, you should make it early in the day and heat it either on top of the stove or in the oven with the roast if there is room. Your dessert should also be made early and be sitting in the refrigerator.

Note: If you like, you may have the butcher cut off the short ribs. Freeze these until you have more from your next roast beef and make Braised Short Ribs.* Weigh the roast again before cooking if the short ribs have been removed.

☞ HAVE ON HAND
  7 pound standing rib roast of beef ("first ribs")
  small cauliflower
  small onions, yellow or white
  Worcestershire sauce
  Parmesan cheese
  small potatoes
  milk or cream
  butter, flour
  bread crumbs
  Lawry's Seasoned Salt
  black peppercorns
  thyme, rosemary and marjoram (optional)

Take the meat out of the refrigerator an hour before cooking. Wipe it with a paper towel. Turn on the oven to 500° if you are searing, to 325° if you are not. Rub the meat with Lawry's Salt and freshly ground black pepper.

Thyme, rosemary and marjoram may also be rubbed in. Put the meat in an open pan in the oven. No water. No basting.

Peel or scrape as many potatoes as you wish and put them in enough lightly salted boiling water to cover. Cook for 10 minutes and drain. Peel 4 or more onions. If you are searing the roast, put the vegetables in the pan when you lower the heat. If you are not searing, put them in half an hour before the meat is done. Turn them occasionally so that they will brown evenly.

Here is the roasting timetable:

Searing: 18 minutes per pound for rare
22 minutes per pound for medium (time includes 20 minutes of searing)

Nonsearing: 22 minutes per pound for rare
25 minutes per pound for medium

If you set the roast, cook it for the first time for 1 hour, whether seared or not. The second time, put it in a 325° oven and cook for 1 hour.

A rolled boned rib roast weighing 5 pounds will give you about the same amount of meat. It will take 10 minutes longer per pound to cook by either method. It should be placed on a rack in the roasting pan and turned occasionally. Since vegetables cannot be browned with this roast, pour off some of the drippings when they collect. Brown the potatoes and onions in this fat in a skillet. A rolled roast may be cooked much more quickly in an electric broiler. Follow the special instructions that came with the machine, but 1 hour usually does it.

I have said nothing about well-done roast beef. If you like it that way, add about 5 minutes per pound.

BRAISED SHORT RIBS WITH VEGETABLES
MIXED GREEN SALAD*
ORANGE ICE*

If you haven't saved up short ribs, you can buy them.
They are inexpensive and make a hearty meal. This dish
takes about 1½ hours to cook, but it may be made a day
ahead of time. It also freezes well.

☞ HAVE ON HAND
    1½ pounds short ribs
    butter or bacon fat
    salt, black peppercorns
    2 medium-sized Irish potatoes
    small onions
    carrots
    thyme, marjoram
    arrowroot flour or cornstarch (optional)

Heat 1½ tablespoons butter or bacon drippings in a
skillet. Brown the short ribs in this over moderate heat.
Sprinkle with 1½ tablespoons salt, freshly ground black
pepper and pinches of thyme and marjoram. Add 1 cup
water, cover and cook slowly for 1 hour. Meanwhile,
scrape or peel the potatoes and cut them in half. Peel 4
or more onions. Scrape 2 carrots and cut them in half. At
the end of an hour, add the vegetables to the meat. Cover
and cook until they are tender, about 30 minutes. If
desired, thicken the sauce by stirring in 1 teaspoon arrowroot flour or cornstarch dissolved in 2 tablespoons cold
water.

⟶⟶❀⟶⟶❀⟶*⟶❀⟶*⟶❀⟶*⟶❀⟶*⟶❀⟶*⟶❀⟶*⟶

> ROLLED BONED SHOULDER OF LAMB
> ARTICHOKES WITH HOLLANDAISE° OR
> PEAS AND CARROTS°
> MASHED POTATOES°
> CODDLING CREAM°

A rolled boned shoulder of lamb is much less expensive than a leg of lamb and is even juicier and tenderer. A 4-pound shoulder will give you enough leftover lamb for Curry* or Barbecued Lamb Hash.* Artichokes,* fresh or frozen, are perfect with lamb as are peas and carrots. There is a bit of gravy, so Mashed Potatoes* are in order.

☞ **HAVE ON HAND**
    4-pound rolled boned shoulder of lamb, no fat inside
    salt, black peppercorns
    Lawry's Seasoned Salt
    rosemary
    onion
    stalk celery
    flour
    2 medium-sized old potatoes
    butter
    cream
    vegetable of your choice

Wipe the shoulder of lamb with paper towels. Season it with ¼ teaspoon Lawry's Salt and 1 tablespoon regular salt, a pinch of rosemary and a generous grinding of black pepper.

Three hours before dinner, put the lamb in a deep iron

casserole which has a cover. Don't cover it yet. Put it in a cold oven and turn the heat to 350°. Put 1 peeled onion and 1 stalk celery in the pot.

In 45 minutes, look and see if the juice is browning. If it is, add ⅓ cup water. If it isn't, wait a bit and add the water when the juice *is* browning. Skim off the fat. Do this with a tablespoon or use the baster. Use either of these implements to baste every 20 minutes, adding ⅓ cup water each time. To baste, you know, means to dip up the juices and pour them over the meat. After the meat has been in the oven for 2 hours, put the lid on the casserole. Half an hour before serving, stir in 1 tablespoon flour mixed with a little cold water.

Remove the strings which were used to tie up the lamb before serving.

ROAST LEG OF LAMB, MINT JELLY
BROWNED POTATOES
PEAS*
ICE CREAM

An evening is going to arrive when one or both sets of parents come to dinner. This would be an easy menu for you to prepare. I won't give you the amounts of potatoes or peas because I don't know how many you will be, but you can figure that out. Make a dessert instead of having ice cream if you feel like it, but get it done early. The peas, as you will remember, can be cooked ahead of time and kept warm on an asbestos pad over low heat. Be sure that

*↩☙↪✱↩☙↪✱↩☙↪✱↩☙↪✱↩☙↪✱↩☙↪✱↩☙↪✱↩☙↪✱↩☙↪✱↩☙↪✱↩

your serving plates are hot and that the lamb is very hot.
There's nothing worse than lukewarm lamb.

☞ HAVE ON HAND
    5- or 6-pound short leg of lamb   mint jelly
    Lawry's Seasoned Salt   small potatoes
    salt, black peppercorns   peas
    garlic (optional)   butter
     rosemary

Preheat the oven to 300°.

Take the meat from the refrigerator, as usual, 1 hour
before cooking. Wipe it with paper towels. Cut gashes in
the fell and insert slivers of garlic. This does not make the
meat taste too garlicky, but it does take away the "furry"
taste. If you do this, rub the meat with regular salt. Otherwise use Lawry's, which has a touch of garlic in it. Rub it
also with freshly ground black pepper and rosemary. The
meat will take about 3 hours to cook. Parboil the potatoes
as for Roast Beef* and put them in with the lamb for the
last half hour.

Place the lamb fell (or fat) side up in an open roasting
pan and roast 30 minutes to the pound for about 3 hours.
If you like lamb pink, cook for a slightly shorter period. Be
sure to let the meat rest in a warm place for 15 minutes
after it's done and before it's carved.

Probably a father or father-in-law will understand the
intricacies of carving a leg of lamb. Otherwise, your beau
had better look at a picture in one of the more compre-
hensive cookbooks. It's easy if you know how, but it's difficult to explain.

Even if both sets of parents are on hand, there will be
leftover lamb. Don't forget how good it is cold.

VEAL CHOPS MAÎTRE D'HÔTEL
CREAMED SPINACH*
NEW POTATOES BROWNED IN THEIR JACKETS
LEMON MERINGUE PIE*

Make the Lemon Meringue Pie* in the morning. As soon as that is baking, make the maître d'hôtel butter. Scrub and parboil the potatoes and cook the chopped spinach according to directions on the box. Always use an enamel or Pyrex saucepan for cooking spinach to avoid a metallic taste. Drain it and chop it again. Cream the spinach* later, while the chops are cooking.

☞ HAVE ON HAND
  2 veal chops cut from the loin, 1 inch thick
  1 box chopped frozen spinach
  new potatoes
  butter
  cream
  lemon
  nutmeg
  salt, black peppercorns
  flour
  parsley

Let ½ stick butter soften. While it does that, chop (cut)* enough parsley to make 1 teaspoon. With a wooden spoon, beat the butter until it is creamy and add

━◦─✺─◦✳◦─✺─◦✳◦─✺─◦✳◦─✺─◦✳◦─✺─◦✳◦─✺─◦✳◦─◦━

the parsley, ¼ teaspoon salt and 1 tablespoon strained
lemon juice. Mix well and put in the refrigerator to
harden. This Maître d'Hôtel butter is good on steak too.

Preheat the oven to 350°.

Take the chops out of the refrigerator. Do I have to go
on telling you this? I don't think so. Sprinkle them with
salt and freshly ground black pepper, and dust them with
flour.

Put 1 tablespoon butter in a skillet over low heat. Add
the potatoes. Shake the pan now and then as they brown.

Dot the chops with butter and put them on the broiling rack 1 inch below the heat. Broil for 8 minutes, turn
and broil 8 minutes on the other side.

Start creaming the spinach.

Transfer the chops to a Pyrex pie plate or shallow baking dish, spread them with a little more butter and put
them back under the broiler. Lower the heat to 200° and
cook 3 minutes on each side, basting a couple of times.
Prick the chops with a fork, and if no pink juice shows,
they are done. Let them rest a few minutes while you
"dish up" the vegetables. Serve with a square of Maître
d'Hôtel butter on each chop.

> **PORK CHOPS**
> **APPLESAUCE**
> **TOMATOES STUFFED WITH CORN***
> **CHOCOLATE MOUSSE***

Later on, you may want to make your own applesauce,
but for now the kind that comes in jars is pretty good.

When you put it in its serving bowl, mix in a little cinnamon or nutmeg to taste. That makes it more like homemade. Fix the Chocolate Mousse* the day before.

☞ **HAVE ON HAND**
> 4 or 6 center-cut loin pork chops cut ½ inch thick
> 1 jar applesauce
> Lawry's Salt, salt, black peppercorns
> rosemary
> 2 medium tomatoes
> buffet-size can whole kernel corn
> small celery heart
> butter
> Parmesan cheese (¼-pound piece)

One hour before dinner (!), take the chops out of the refrigerator and season them with Lawry's Salt, a grinding of black pepper and a pinch of rosemary. If the chops are very fat, cut some off and reserve it.

Preheat the oven to 350° for the tomatoes* and get them ready. They will take 30 minutes to bake.

When the tomatoes go into the oven, put the fat from the chops in an iron skillet. Turn on the heat, high, and when there is a little melted fat in the skillet, remove the solid pieces and put in the chops. If the chops haven't much fat on them, take one and rub its fat side over the hot pan to grease it just a little and then put the chops in. Sear them on both sides. That is, get them nice and brown over high heat. Lower the heat and cook slowly for 20 minutes.

```
┌─────────────────────────────────────────────┐
│                                               │
│              PORK  TENDERLOIN                 │
│           SPICY SQUASH CASSEROLE*             │
│       APPLE PIE* OR APPLES BONNE FEMME*       │
│                                               │
└─────────────────────────────────────────────┘
```

This is one of the most delicious cuts of pork. When it is cooked this simple but unusual way, applesauce is not needed. The Spicy Squash Casserole* goes beautifully with it. Fix dessert ahead of time or even the day before.

☞ HAVE ON HAND

   1 pound pork tenderloin cut into 4 patties, flattened out
   bacon
   1 large or 2 small tomatoes
   1 large onion
   salt, black peppercorns
   1 box frozen squash
   butter
   powdered ginger
   brown sugar

Preheat oven to 350°.

Spread 8 strips of bacon to form 4 crosses. Put 1 pork patty, lightly salted and peppered, in the middle of each cross. Top each patty with a ½-inch slice of onion, peeled of course, and on top of that put a ½-inch slice of tomato. Cross the bacon strips over the whole arrangement and fasten with toothpicks. Place in an iron skillet and cook over moderate heat for a few minutes until the bottom sides are brown. Add ½ cup water and cook, uncovered, in the oven for 1 hour.

Fix the squash and put it in the oven with the pork for the last half hour.

```
┌─────────────────────────────────────┐
│                                       │
│            SPARERIBS                   │
│         BRUSSELS SPROUTS*              │
│          SWEET POTATOES                │
│          APRICOT WHIP*                 │
│                                       │
└─────────────────────────────────────┘
```

Buy fresh meaty, loin spareribs and have the butcher crack them or cut them into sections. They may be baked plain or basted with barbecue sauce.

☞ **HAVE ON HAND**
    2 pounds spareribs
    salt, black peppercorns, rosemary or sage
    lemon and onion or barbecue sauce
    1 box frozen Brussels sprouts
    cream
    butter
    nutmeg
    2 sweet potatoes

Preheat the oven to 350°. Take the ribs out of the refrigerator, wipe them with paper towels, and season with salt, freshly ground black pepper and either sage or rosemary. Both are good.

Fix the Brussels sprouts.* Boil the sweet potatoes if you are going to have them mashed* and the ribs barbecued. If the ribs are to be plain, parboil the potatoes (cook them for 15 minutes in boiling salted water to cover), drain, and brown them with the ribs during the last half hour of cooking.

Put the ribs in a shallow pan with several slices of lemon and several slices of onion on them if you are having them plain. Put them in the oven 1½ hours before dinner. Turn them occasionally and baste them either with barbecue sauce or with the pan juices.

HAM SLICE
LEAF SPINACH
POUND CAKE*

There are many ways to bake a slice of tenderized ham. It may be covered with 1½ cups of cider, pineapple juice, grape juice, cranberry juice, coffee, ginger ale, or milk. No matter how you cook it, the fat should be removed and the ham should be soaked in cold water for at least an hour. Cooking time is also an hour. This particular menu does not seem to me to call for potatoes, but have them if you wish. Leaf spinach gets along with it very well.

☞ **HAVE ON HAND**
    1 slice tenderized ham weighing 1 pound, cut as thick as
        possible
    prepared mustard
    light brown sugar
    buffet-size can crushed pineapple
    1 box frozen leaf spinach
    lemon or wine vinegar
    butter

Preheat oven to 300°.

Put the soaked ham in a shallow baking dish. Spread the top and sides with 1 teaspoon mustard and sprinkle with ¼ cup firmly packed brown sugar. Drain the can of pineapple and reserve the juice. Spread the pineapple on the ham. Add enough water to the juice to make ½ cup. Pour this over the ham. Bake for 1 hour.

Cook the spinach according to directions on the box, drain very thoroughly, butter lightly, and serve with lemon wedges or wine vinegar.

The Pound Cake* may be made by you or bought.

SPICED HAM BUTT
CREAMED SPINACH*
MASHED SWEET POTATOES*
CHEESE AND FRUIT

Buy a small smoked shoulder butt weighing not much more than 1½ pounds. You will have some ham left over to make croquettes or sandwiches, or to mince and put in an omelet. If you follow my suggestion about dessert, be sure to take the cheese out of the refrigerator some time before dinner and be equally sure to leave the fruit in it. The idea is ice-cold fruit and soft warm cheese.

☞ **HAVE ON HAND**
    1 small smoked shoulder butt
    onion
    cloves
    bay leaf

stick cinnamon
celery seed
light brown sugar
flour
cider vinegar
1 box frozen spinach
cream
butter
salt, black peppercorns
nutmeg
2 sweet potatoes

Cover the ham with cold water. Add 1 medium onion, peeled and sliced, 3 whole cloves, 1 bay leaf, 1 stick cinnamon and ¼ teaspoon celery seed. Cover tightly and simmer for 2 hours or until tender. Remove ham from water and place in a shallow baking dish. Preheat oven to 350°. Spread ham with a mixture of ¼ cup firmly packed brown sugar, 1 tablespoon vinegar and 1 tablespoon flour. Bake for 15 minutes. The ham may be boiled the day before. Otherwise, fix the spinach* and the sweet potatoes* while it is boiling.

LIVER AND BACON
BUTTERED ONIONS*
HASHED BROWN POTATOES*
FRUIT TARTS*

If you follow this menu, the dinner will be predominately beige and brown, so be colorful in the dessert department. A green salad* at some point would not be amiss. It occurs to me that you might prefer smothered onions* with liver instead of bacon. In that case, have green beans* or broccoli* or asparagus,* and cook the liver in butter.

☞ HAVE ON HAND
   4 or 6 thin slices calves' liver
   bacon
   boiling onions or 1 jar boiled onions
   butter
   Lawry's Seasoned Salt, paprika
   2 medium-sized Irish potatoes
   salt, black peppercorns

   Boil the potatoes for Hashed Browned Potatoes* and let them cool. When you hash and brown them, omit the onions this time.
   Peel and boil the onions.* Take the liver and bacon out of the refrigerator.
   Half an hour before dinner, cook the bacon.* Wash the liver, dry it with paper towels and sprinkle it with Lawry's salt and lots of paprika. Finish the vegetables and keep them hot.
   When the bacon is finished, drain off most of the fat but leave a little. Have the heat moderate. Add 1 generous tablespoon butter, and when it sizzles put in the liver. A couple of minutes on each side is sufficient if you like liver pink. Give the first side 2 minutes, turn, cook 2 minutes, and prick with a fork. If a little blood shows, it is pink. Cook a little longer if you prefer, but not much. Overcooking makes liver hard.

❋⚘❋⚘❋⚘❋⚘❋⚘❋⚘❋⚘❋⚘❋⚘❋⚘❋⚘❋⚘

BROILED SWEETBREADS WITH BACON
PEAS À LA FRANÇAISE*
PARSLEY POTATOES*
CHANTILLY MOUSSE*

Veal sweetbreads are a great delicacy and are apt to be expensive, but they are worth it. A little more than half a pound will serve two. Each sweetbread has two sections, heart and lung. Try to get two heart sections. They are easier to handle. There are many ways to fix sweetbreads, as you will discover. I am suggesting that you broil them because it's easy and also because you might like to use them in a mixed grill sometime instead of sausages. No matter how you cook them, they must always be parboiled, as they are here. This may be done the day before. The final cooking takes no time at all, so have the vegetables ready before you put the sweetbreads in the broiler. The dessert, of course, will have been made the day before. If you have parboiled the sweetbreads and if you should be in a rush, skip the potatoes, use canned peas, and you can have dinner ready in about 20 minutes.

☞ **HAVE ON HAND**
     ½ pound veal sweetbreads or more (2 heart sections)
     bacon
     salt, black peppercorns
     butter
     lemon
     parsley
     new potatoes

1 package frozen peas or 1 can No. 1 Sift Early June
    Peas
little white onions
lettuce
sugar, nutmeg

Take the sweetbreads out of their wrappings as soon as they arrive and put them in a bowl of ice water for at least 20 minutes — longer if possible.

Have enough water in a saucepan to cover them, but don't put them in yet. Add 2 tablespoons lemon juice and ½ teaspoon salt to the water and let it come to a boil. Add the sweetbreads, lower the heat, and simmer 20 minutes. Take them out, drain them, and plunge them into the ice water. When they are chilled and firm, drain them and carefully remove the thin membrane that covers them and all bits of tubes and hard stuff that you can see. If you are not using them right away, cover them and put them in the refrigerator.

Preheat the oven to 400°. Cook the bacon.* Fix the vegetables.

Melt 2 tablespoons butter. Slice the sweetbreads horizontally. Using a pastry brush or your fingers, cover the sweetbreads with butter on all sides. Sprinkle them with salt and freshly ground black pepper and put them on a rack under the broiler or, as directed, in the electric broiler. When they are delicately brown, in about 2 or 3 minutes, turn them and brush with butter again. They will only take 5 minutes, in all, to cook. Serve them with strips of bacon beside them.

Poultry

HOW TO SHOP FOR POULTRY

Chickens and turkeys are available whole, halved or by the piece, fresh or quick-frozen. Cold-storage birds are also obtainable, but please don't buy them. They have lost flavor, and no matter what you do to them you cannot achieve the crisp outside and juicy inside which are the joys of roasted, broiled or fried poultry. The way to identify a cold-storage bird is by the skin. If it is white and rubbery, that's it. Pass by.

Fresh-killed chickens, turkeys or ducks are, of course, the best. Choose chickens with plump breasts and smooth skin. In younger birds, those used for broiling and frying, the skin should be soft and thin, the breastbone soft and pliable. These young birds weigh in the neighborhood of 2 pounds. Roasting chickens weigh from 3½ to 5 pounds. The breastbone should still be pliable, the skin clear, and the legs smooth. Older chickens, known as fowl, have thicker skin and a hard breastbone, and they weigh from

4 to 6 pounds. They are excellent for fricassee, stew, soup, creamed dishes and salads.

A good turkey should have the same characteristics as a good roasting chicken: a plump breast, smooth skin and a flexible breastbone. Turkeys are now available weighing as little as 4 pounds, a good size for a small family.

Both ducks and geese should be young, plump and heavy. Young ducks weigh from 3 to 5 pounds, young geese from 8 to 10. A 3½-pound duck will feed two generously.

Don't forget the little birds. Squab, which is expensive, is a lovely treat if you like its tender dark flesh. Cornish game hens are no longer as high-priced as they were when they first appeared on the market. They are usually sold quick-frozen, and you can even find them already stuffed and ready for the oven.

Always have the butcher cut out the oil sac at the base of the tail no matter what kind of poultry you are buying.

When you get poultry home from the store, look to see if all the pinfeathers are out. If not, pull them out with tweezers. Hold the bird over a gas flame or light a piece of rolled newspaper and singe off the fine hairs. Let cold water run through the bird (unless, of course, it is a pre-stuffed game hen), but do not soak it. Dry it with paper towels.

FRIED CHICKEN
GREEN BEANS* OR BROCCOLI,* BROWNED BUTTER*
RICE*
FRUIT COMPOTE* AND CAKE*

❊⤳☙❊⤳☙❊⤳☙❊⤳☙❊⤳☙❊⤳☙❊⤳☙❊⤳☙❊⤳☙❊⤳

Most married couples seem to be divided, and happily
so, on the subject of white and dark meat. If this is the
case in your family, buy one chicken breast and two legs.
If *he* is a hearty eater, get more of whichever he likes. Of
course, if you'd like to have some cold fried chicken left
over for nibbling purposes, get a 2-pound fryer cut up.
The chicken will take about an hour to cook, and you have
to be around. Fix the Fruit Compote* in the morning or
the day before. Feel like making a cake? It might be fun.
There are two recipes back yonder.

☞**HAVE ON HAND**
> 2-pound frying chicken, cut up, or chicken pieces
> flour
> Lawry's Seasoned Salt
> salt, black peppercorns
> marjoram or tarragon
> Crisco or other vegetable shortening
> butter
> half-and-half (half milk, half cream)
> 1 pound broccoli or ½ pound green beans or 1 package
>   of either, frozen
> rice (any kind)

Choose a heavy skillet just big enough to hold your
chicken pieces comfortably.

Put ¼ cup flour, ¼ teaspoon Lawry's Salt, 1 teaspoon
regular salt, a grinding of black pepper and a pinch of marjoram or tarragon in a paper bag. Put the chicken in the
bag, twist the open end, and shake the bag so that all the
pieces will be coated with seasoned flour.

Heat ⅓ cup vegetable shortening and ½ stick butter in

＊＊＊＊＊＊＊＊＊＊＊＊＊＊＊＊＊＊＊＊＊＊＊＊

the skillet over moderate heat. When it is bubbling, add
the chicken, cover the pan, and reduce the heat to low.
After 20 minutes, turn the chicken, cover again, and cook
for another 20 minutes. Take the lid off and turn the heat
up to a little better than moderate. Turn the pieces as they
cook for a few more minutes until they are golden brown
on all sides.

Take the chicken out of the pan and keep it warm in a
shallow pan lined with paper towels, in a 200° oven.

Stir 1 tablespoon flour into the pan juices and add 1
cup half-and-half. Simmer over low heat, stirring, until
thick and smooth. Taste and season, if necessary, with salt
and pepper. Serve the gravy in a sauce boat.

I'm sure I don't have to tell you that you have plenty
of time to cook the vegetable and rice* while the chicken
is frying.

BROILED CHICKEN, CURRANT JELLY
ASPARAGUS, BROWNED BUTTER°
SCALLOPED POTATOES°
SABAYON SAUCE° WITH FRUIT

If you have an electric broiler, you'll want to try broiling
your chicken in that, using the recipe in the booklet that
came with it. I prefer chicken broiled the old-fashioned
way, so that's the recipe I'm going to give you. Because
cooking time is about 1½ hours and the chicken must be

✽⤙☙⤚✽⤙☙⤚✽⤙☙⤚✽⤙☙⤚✽⤙☙⤚✽⤙☙⤚✽⤙☙⤚✽⤙☙⤚✽⤙☙⤚

basted every 15 minutes, don't plan to take a nap while it's
cooking. As a matter of fact, that's why I suggested
Sabayon* for dessert. You can make that while you're at-
tending to the chicken. The Scalloped Potatoes* go into
the oven a half hour after the chicken has started and will
be done at the same time.

☞HAVE ON HAND
        2- to 2½-pound broiler, split
        butter
        Lawry's Seasoned Salt
        black peppercorns, paprika
        2 medium-sized Irish potatoes
        milk
        1 pound fresh asparagus or 1 box frozen

Preheat the oven to 300°.

Get the potatoes ready to be put in the oven.

Wash the chicken giblets and freeze them, keeping the
liver separate.

Melt ½ stick butter and brush the chicken with it on all
sides. Rub it with Lawry's Salt, freshly ground black pepper and plenty of paprika. Put the chicken, skin side up,
in a flat baking dish as far away from the broiling element
as possible. Leave the door open if your stove is electric,
ajar if it's gas. Baste every 15 minutes with the juices in
the pan.

After a half hour of cooking, add ¼ cup water and continue to baste with this. If the chicken weighs under 2
pounds, it may be done in less than 1½ hours. Test by
pricking with a fork. If there is any pink in the juice, it is
not yet done. Another test is to move the drumstick. If it
moves easily, the chicken is done.

```
ROAST CHICKEN OR TURKEY
BRUSSELS SPROUTS IN CREAM*
SPICY SQUASH CASSEROLE* OR MASHED SWEET
POTATOES*
MINCE* OR PUMPKIN PIE*
```

The easiest and, to my mind, best way to roast a chicken or a turkey is in aluminum foil; after seasoning it and stuffing it if you wish, you just wrap it up, stick it in the oven, and forget about it until 20 minutes before it's done. The vegetables may be prepared early in the day and heated up, the Brussels sprouts* on top of the stove and the squash* or sweet potatoes* under the broiler.

☞ HAVE ON HAND
    4-pound roasting chicken or 4- to 6-pound turkey
    aluminum foil (wide)
    butter
    salt, black peppercorns, paprika
    poultry seasoning
    lemon
    1 pint Brussels sprouts or 1 box frozen
    cream
    1 box frozen squash or 2 medium-sized sweet potatoes
    brown sugar
    ginger (for squash)
    1 bag poultry stuffing (if desired)
    onion
    stalk celery
    parsley
    bay leaf

❋〜❀〜❀〜❀〜❀〜❀〜❀〜❀〜❀〜❀〜❀〜❀〜❀〜❀〜❀〜

Preheat the oven to 325°.

Wipe the bird with a damp cloth or a cut lemon. Rinse with cold water and pat dry with paper towels. Season both cavities with salt, freshly ground black pepper and poultry seasoning.

I suggest that, as a beginner, you use commercial stuffing. It is very good. Follow the directions on the bag, making the stuffing moist or dry, according to your taste. Don't use too much, since the bird should be stuffed loosely.

Stuff the wishbone cavity first and skewer the neck skin to the back. Shape wings akimbo style, bring tips onto back.

Place the bird breast down in a deep bowl. Spoon stuffing into the body cavity. Shake the bird to settle the dressing; don't pack it in. Place skewers across the opening and lace shut with cord or heavy thread. Tie drumsticks securely to tail.

Rub the outside of the chicken or turkey with 1 tablespoon soft butter, 1 teaspoon salt and 1 teaspoon paprika. Put a large piece of aluminum foil on a shallow pan. Place the bird in the center. Put extra pieces of foil over the wing tips and the ends of the legs. Bring the foil up, overlapping on the breast by 3 inches. Press foil down on the body and close open ends by folding the underneath foil up and over the top foil. Place in the oven. A 4- to 6-pound chicken or turkey will take 3 to 3½ hours. (For future reference, an 8- to 12-pound turkey will take 4 to 4½ hours.) Since you don't even have to look at it while it's cooking, you have plenty of time to fix the vegetables if you haven't done so earlier, and to put the filling in the pie shell.

Half an hour before the bird is done, open the foil and turn it back so that the meat may brown. Pour the drippings from the foil into a saucepan. Fifteen minutes later, move the drumstick up and down; the leg joint should give easily if the bird is about done. It's a good idea to start cooking a turkey or chicken about 30 minutes ahead of schedule to avoid delay, should it take longer to cook than estimated. This also allows time for it to rest and for you to make gravy if you wish to.

Giblet Gravy

For the gravy, after the bird is in the oven, wash the giblets and the neck. Remove the fat from the gizzard and the heart. Put the giblets and the neck in a fairly deep saucepan with a small peeled onion, a stalk of celery (chopped), a sprig of parsley (cut up), a bay leaf, ½ teaspoon salt and enough cold water to cover. Simmer slowly, uncovered, for 1 hour. Remove the liver after a half hour and reserve it. Strain the broth. Pick the meat from the neck and chop it and the giblets, including the liver.

When you have poured the drippings from the aluminum foil, skim off the fat and save 1 tablespoonful. Put this in a small heavy saucepan and add 1 scant tablespoon flour. Cook and stir, over moderate heat, until flour becomes golden brown. Stir in 1 cup of the strained giblet broth. Cook and stir until smooth and fairly thick. Season to taste with salt and freshly ground black pepper and add the chopped giblets.

If you aren't going to make gravy, make the broth anyway, saving the liver as usual for other purposes. The broth can be stored in the refrigerator for several days or can be frozen. It may be used whenever chicken broth or stock is called for.

CHICKEN GRITTI
PEAS*
LIME ICE AND BLUEBERRIES

This dish is a specialty at the Gritti Palace Hotel in Venice. If you want to serve it to two guests, double the amount of sauce and cheese, but if you want to be economical, you can reap three good meals for two people from one bird as follows: Have your favorite parts à la Gritti the first night; make Croquettes* out of the rest and freeze them; make a Risotto,* using the broth, for a third supper. Peas,* fresh, frozen or canned, are the perfect vegetable for this rather elaborate dish. Potatoes are not needed because noodles are involved. The lime ice that I suggest is "boughten." Blueberries are lovely with it.

☞ **HAVE ON HAND**
      3-pound fowl, quartered
      1 can clear chicken broth
      salt, black peppercorns, white pepper
      parsley
      onion
      Parmesan cheese (¼ pound in one piece)
      light cream
      milk
      butter, flour
      ½ recipe Hollandaise Sauce*
      8-ounce package broad noodles
      1 package frozen peas

Wipe the pieces of chicken with a damp cloth and put them in a deep saucepan or small pot. Wash the giblets, remove fat, and put them in the pot, except for the liver. Wash it, wrap it up, and freeze it. Pour 1 can chicken broth over the chicken and add enough cold water so that the pieces are covered. Put a lid on the pot, bring to a boil over moderate heat, lower the heat, and simmer. After about 10 minutes, remove the lid briefly while you skim off the froth with a large tablespoon. This is called "scumming." Add 1 teaspoon salt, a grinding of black pepper, a sprig of cut parsley, and a small peeled onion. Put the cover back on and simmer until the chicken is tender. This will take 45 minutes to 1 hour.

While the chicken is cooking, grate enough Parmesan cheese to make 4 tablespoons.

Make ½ recipe Hollandaise Sauce.*

Then make ½ cup cheese (Mornay) sauce as follows: Melt 1 tablespoon butter in a small, preferably enamellined iron, saucepan. (Iron is best for a sauce like this which needs long cooking because you don't have to stir it constantly as you do in a thinner pan.) Have ½ cup milk heating in a measuring cup or saucepan on an asbestos pad over low heat. When the butter has melted, stir in 1 tablespoon flour, using a wooden spoon. When the roux* is smooth, add the hot milk gradually. Season with a dash of salt and a pinch of white pepper. Add ½ cup light cream and simmer 5 minutes, stirring occasionally. Add 3 tablespoons of the cheese and simmer for another 5 minutes. Remove from the heat and, stirring constantly, add 1 tablespoon butter and the Hollandaise.

✳〜✿〜✳〜✿〜✳〜✿〜✳〜✿〜✳〜✿〜✳〜✿〜✳〜✿〜✳〜✿〜✳〜✿〜✳〜

Put the sauce in a warm place but not over hot water or
even low heat.

Turn on the oven to 400°.

Now get 1 quart of water boiling in a sizable pot. Add
1 teaspoon salt, and when the water is boiling madly,
add ½ box broad noodles. Cook according to the instructions on the box, about 9 to 12 minutes. When they are
done, drain them in a colander, add a scant tablespoon
butter, and toss them with a fork. Put the colander over
hot water so the noodles will keep warm.

When the chicken is done, spread the noodles in a
shallow baking dish and arrange the pieces of chicken on
top. Put the other pieces in the refrigerator. Strain the
broth and refrigerate it. Cover the chicken and noodles
with the sauce, sprinkle with the rest of the cheese, and
put under the broiler for 7 minutes. It will come out
nicely browned.

TWO ROAST DUCKS
SPICY SQUASH CASSEROLE*
PEAS*
WILD RICE
MINCE PIE* OR PLUM PUDDING

Some ovens can hold two ducks but not one 7- to
8-pound turkey. A friend of mine who lives in a small
apartment in New York and has such an oven solved
Christmas dinner for four by cooking two ducks, each in
a different manner. The farmhouse-style duck was eaten
first, and the delicate and aromatic duck a l'orange fol-

lowed it. The squash was served with the first duck
and plain peas with the second. The rice, which goes
with each, need not be wild, if it is too expensive. There
are several interestingly flavored rices available; one, for
instance, tastes like popcorn, and one tastes rather like
wild rice. Either of these would do. Applesauce should
be served with duck No. 1; nothing with duck No. 2. If
you decide on Mince Pie,* heat it in the oven after the
ducks come out. Plum puddings come in various size
cans. A one-pounder serves four. Hard Sauce* goes with
either mince pie or plum pudding.

Of course, you don't necessarily have to have two ducks.
If you are alone, have one cooked either way.

DUCK FARMHOUSE-STYLE

☞ **HAVE ON HAND**

3- to 3½-pound duck	sage
1 cooking apple	bread crumbs
yellow onions	salt, black peppercorns
½ pound sausage meat	Lawry's Seasoned Salt
1 package frozen squash	ginger
light brown sugar	butter

Preheat oven to 325°.

Take care of pinfeathers and fine hairs in the usual
way. Rinse the duck with cold running water and pat
dry with paper towels. Rub it inside and out with Lawry's
Salt and freshly ground black pepper.

Peel and mince 1 small yellow onion. Cook the sausage
meat over moderate heat in an iron skillet with a pinch
of sage. Stir it with a fork as it cooks. When it is brown,
remove it from the pan with a slotted spoon. Cook the

minced onion in the fat left in the sausage pan; stir over
moderate heat, until golden brown. While the onion
cooks, wash and core the apple and dice it, unpeeled.
Turn off the heat under the onion and add to the onion
the apple, the sausage meat and ½ cup bread crumbs.
Season to taste with salt and freshly ground black pepper.
Put a little stuffing in the wishbone cavity and fasten the
neck skin to the back with skewers. Put the duck in a
deep bowl breast down, and put the rest of the stuffing
in the body cavity. Shake to settle the stuffing. Skewer
the opening closed or lace it as in Roast Chicken.* Put
the duck on a rack in an open roasting pan and prick
the skin all over so that the fat under the skin will melt,
leaving the skin crisp. Roast for 1½ to 2 hours, depending
on whether you like duck well-done or not. Pour or siphon
off (with the baster) the accumulated fat from time to
time. Prick the skin occasionally also.

If you would prefer not to stuff the duck, season it
the same way and put 1 quartered apple, 1 quartered
onion and some celery leaves in the body cavity. Roast
in the same manner. Whichever way you cook it, don't
forget to let it rest before carving.

DUCK A L'ORANGE

☞ HAVE ON HAND
        3- to 3½-pound duck
        2 California or navel oranges
        dry white wine
        cornstarch or arrowroot flour
        salt, black peppercorns
        1 package frozen peas
        butter

Rinse the duck as in the prevous recipe and dry it. Rub it inside and out with salt and freshly ground black pepper. Put ½ sliced orange, unpeeled, in the body cavity and skewer the opening shut. Roast the duck in the same manner as the first one.

Squeeze the other half of the orange you put in the duck. Pare the zest, or outer skin, from the second orange, using a very sharp knife. You don't want any of the white that lies between the flesh of the orange and the skin. Cut the peel into tiny, thin strips and parboil them for 3 minutes, that is, plunge them into boiling water, lower the heat, and simmer. Divide the peeled orange into sections. Remove all membranes and set the sections aside.

When the duck is done, remove it from the pan and keep it warm.

Pour off most of the fat from the roasting pan. Scrape the pan with a big spoon and put 2 tablespoons of duck juice and fat, which is what you'll get, into a small saucepan. Add ½ cup boiling water and that ½ cup orange juice. Add 1 cup dry white wine into which you have mixed 1 scant tablespoon arrowroot flour or cornstarch. Stir until thick. Add the strips of orange peel, season to taste, and serve hot, in a sauce boat. Garnish the duck with the orange sections.

About the giblets — make giblet gravy for plain roast duck or for duck farmhouse-style in the same manner as you make it for Roast Chicken.* Otherwise, freeze the giblets, wrapping the liver separately for use later in an omelet or in Salmi of Duck.*

> ## ROAST SQUABS OR
> ## ROAST ROCK CORNISH GAME HENS
> ## PEAS*
> ## GLACÉED FRUIT TARTS*

Neither of these birds is fat, so they need "larding" as well as basting. Larding, in this case, means putting a thin slice of salt pork over the breasts. Ask the butcher to do this. Peas are the classic accompaniment for squab, and since they are equally good with game hen, I suggest them here. If you would rather have something else, go right ahead. Make the tarts in the morning or the day before. The peas may be fixed while the birds are cooking, since you must be around to baste. They take only 45 minutes to roast, however, and about 15 minutes to stuff. Incidentally, stuffing them is not mandatory. Personally, I prefer squabs unstuffed. Suit yourself.

☞ HAVE ON HAND

> 2 squab or 2 medium-sized Rock Cornish game hens, larded
> 1 pound peas or 1 box frozen or 1 can No. 1 Sift Early June peas
> rice (wild, brown or your choice for stuffing)
> onion (for stuffing)
> butter
> salt, black peppercorns, poultry seasoning
> dry white wine or dry vermouth
> watercress

Preheat the oven to 400°.

If you want to stuff the birds, cook slightly less than ¼ cup rice.* Mince enough onion to make 1 teaspoonful. Sauté this in 1 tablespoon butter until light golden in color. Wash the livers from the birds, dry them with paper towels, and add them to the onion. Stir with a fork. After about 3 minutes, turn off the heat and chop the livers in the pan. You can do this with a chopper or with a knife and fork. Mix the livers and onions with the cooked rice.

Rub the birds inside and out with salt, freshly ground black pepper, a scant teaspoonful of poultry seasoning and soft butter. Stuff the body cavity and skewer the opening closed. Twist the wings akimbo-style behind the back and tie the legs together. Put the pieces of salt pork back on the breasts. Put the birds in the oven in a shallow baking dish.

Melt 1 generous tablespoon butter and add it to ⅓ cup warm dry white wine or vermouth. After 15 minutes, turn the oven down to 300° and baste the birds with the wine and butter. Cook until tender, testing in the usual way by moving the drumsticks. Baste every now and then. The cooking will take about a half hour; the squab may take a little longer than the game hens. When the wine-and-butter mix gives out, baste with the pan juices. Garnish with watercress.

Fish

For a family of two, such as yours, fish steaks or fillets, scallops or shrimp are apt to be what you usually buy. Be sure that these smell fresh. If, on occasion, you buy a whole fish, select one with bright eyes, red gills, and firm flesh. It should smell fresh too, of course.

There are six basic ways to cook fish. Those that you, with a small family, are most apt to use are sautéeing, poaching, frying, and broiling. So, instead of giving you a group of specific recipes for different kinds of fish, I shall explain these four methods and indicate the types of fish to which they apply. Remember one thing: Fish, as opposed to meat, poultry or practically anything else, is not cooked in order to make it tender but simply to bring out its flavor. Therefore never overcook it.

SAUTÉED FISH

To sauté is to cook in butter, and fish cooked this way is called "à la Meunière." Small fish, slices of fish or fish fillets take to this treatment; small whole trout, slices of halibut or swordfish, fillets of flounder, sole or perch, scallops and shad roe are your best bets. One pound of fish serves two. Good accompaniments for sautéed fish are stewed tomatoes, green beans, new potatoes, cucumbers in sour cream, or mixed vegetable salad.

If the **fish** is frozen, defrost it completely before cooking. Pat dry with paper towels. Season it with **salt** and freshly **ground black pepper.** Sprinkle it with **flour.** Have **2 tablespoons butter** bubbling in a skillet large enough to hold the fish. Put the fish in the pan and cook, over moderate heat, until delicately browned on the underside. Turn it with a spatula and brown the other side. Remove the fish to a warm platter, sprinkle it with **lemon juice** and surround it with **chopped parsley** and **lemon wedges.** Add a scant tablespoon butter to the **juices in the pan** and let it brown a little. Pour this over the fish.

Blanched and **slivered almonds** may be browned in the butter. Buy these by the quarter pound and keep them in a tightly covered jar. Use ⅓ cup for 2 servings. The fish is then called "Amandine."

Another thing you can do is to let the butter (without almonds) brown until it is almost black. This is called "beurre noir" and has a special taste, which you may like.

POACHED FISH

To poach is to simmer in liquid. It is the most delicate way to cook fish, but if you do it you must be prepared to make a sauce. For your purposes the kinds of fish best suited to poaching are fillets of sole, flounder or halibut, and salmon or turbot steaks. The poaching is the same for each, but certain sauces are best with certain fish.

*⟶❀⟶✳⟶❀⟶✳⟶❀⟶✳⟶❀⟶✳⟶❀⟶✳⟶❀⟶✳⟶❀⟶✳⟶❀⟶✳⟶❀⟶✳⟶

The sauces will follow. Tiny peas, asparagus and new
potatoes all go well with poached fish.

Butter a shallow baking dish. Season **2 fillets or 2 steaks**
with **salt** and freshly **ground black pepper.** Put them in
the dish and sprinkle with the **juice of ½ lemon.** Add
½ cup dry white wine or dry vermouth. Water may be
substituted, but wine is much better. Cover tightly with
aluminum foil and bring to a boil over moderate heat.
This will take only a minute or two. Lift an edge of the
foil and peek. As soon as the liquid is boiling, lower the
heat as far as it will go and simmer for 8 minutes. Remove the fish to a warm platter and cover it with foil.
Strain the juices remaining in the dish into a bowl if
you are cooking sole, flounder or halibut. You will need
them for:

WHITE WINE SAUCE FOR SOLE,
FLOUNDER OR HALIBUT

Melt **1 tablespoon butter** in a saucepan and stir in
1 tablespoon flour. When this roux* is smooth, stir in
the **hot fish stock** gradually. Cook and stir it until thick.
Thin with **a little cream.** Season to taste with **salt** and
pepper. Pour the sauce over the fish, garnish with **parsley,**
and serve. Ice-cold seedless green grapes may be spread
over the fish before the sauce is poured on it. The dish
is then called "Véronique" and has lovely contrasts in
taste and temperature. Instead of grapes, ¼ pound washed
and sliced mushrooms may be spread over the fish while
it is poaching. Remove them with the fish and then add
them to the sauce.

BÉARNAISE SAUCE

This wonderful sauce is, in this case, for salmon, but it is famous for its relationship with steak. Salmon may also be served with Hollandaise Sauce.*

Put ½ cup dry white wine, 1 tablespoon tarragon vinegar, 1 teaspoon minced onion, 1 teaspoon minced parsley, a grinding of black pepper, and a pinch of tarragon in a saucepan. Cook, uncovered, over moderate heat until there is only about ¼ cup liquid remaining. Strain, cool and proceed as with Hollandaise,* using this liquid instead of lemon juice.

SAUCE MOUSSELINE

This is simply half Hollandaise,* and half whipped cream. Use it for halibut or turbot.

SAUCE VERTE

This is green mayonnaise and is designed to accompany cold poached salmon. The combination is a marriage made in heaven and should be washed down with a small bottle of chilled white wine. Treat yourselves some summer evening.

Wash and chop 3 or 4 spinach leaves, ½ bunch watercress, and 3 or 4 sprigs parsley. Add 1 teaspoon chopped chives. Put through a food mill or swirl in an electric blender with 1 teaspoon lemon juice. Strain into 1 cup mayonnaise. Mix well.

FRIED FISH

Only very small fish, fillets or thin slices of fish should be fried. If the fish is thick, it may get dry on the outside before it is done inside. Smelts, scallops, butterfish, fillets of pike and haddock or slices of halibut are good when done this way. Tartar sauce, which you might as well buy, is the sauce for fried fish. Stewed tomatoes* or creamed spinach* go nicely with it, as do Cucumbers in Sour Cream.* Potatoes* should be boiled or mashed.

Beat 1 egg with a fork and mix it with 1 tablespoon milk. Dip the pieces of fish in this and then roll them in bread crumbs. Have ½ cup peanut oil bubbling in a skillet. Add the fish and cook quickly, over moderate heat, until golden brown on both sides. Serve garnished with parsley and lemon wedges.

BROILED FISH

For broiling, fillets of sole, white fish, flounder, or haddock, steaks of halibut, salmon or swordfish are your choices. Once again, stewed tomatoes* are the best accompaniment.

Preheat the oven to 450°.

Brush the fillets or steaks with peanut oil or melted butter and put them in a shallow, buttered baking dish. Put the dish in the broiler, 2 inches from the heat. Brown the fish on both sides and reduce the heat to 350°. Baste with 2 tablespoons melted butter to which a little Lawry's Salt and freshly ground black pepper have been added, and, if you like, a pinch of dill, basil or tarragon. Cook 12 to 20 minutes in all, depending on the thickness of the fish. If you find that you cannot turn the fish, don't. Just baste. When the fish flakes easily with a fork, it is done. Serve with lemon butter, made by adding ½ tablespoon lemon juice to 2 tablespoons soft butter.

TUNA FISH OR SALMON CASSEROLE

This recipe and the one following are the two excep-
tios to my rule of no specific recipes for specific fish.
I am including them because they are good and because
they are a change of pace. Have a salad of cucumbers,
tomatoes, watercress and lettuce with this dish and follow
it with a dessert like Apples Bonne Femme.*

☞ HAVE ON HAND
   flour
   milk or half-and-half
   butter
   lemon juice or dry sherry
   bread crumbs
   7-ounce can tuna fish or salmon
   salt, black peppercorns, paprika

Preheat the oven to 400°.

First make the cream sauce. Put 1 cup milk or half-
and-half in a saucepan or a measuring cup over low heat.
Melt 1 tablespoon butter in an iron saucepan over moderate heat and stir in 1 tablespoon flour. Lower the heat
and stir until the roux* is smooth. Add the hot liquid and
stir until thick and smooth. Add salt, freshly ground black
pepper and paprika to taste. If you are using an iron
saucepan, keep stirring until the pan cools off a bit. Iron
retains heat, and the sauce goes on cooking for a minute
or two. Stir in 1 tablespoon lemon juice or 1 tablespoon
dry sherry.

Melt 2 tablespoons butter and mix with 1 cup bread
crumbs.

Open the can of tuna fish or salmon and put the contents in a casserole or baking dish about 7 inches in diameter. Mix the cream sauce with the fish. Spread with the buttered crumbs and bake for approximately 20 minutes or until brown and bubbly.

BROILED ROCK LOBSTER TAILS

If your freezer compartment is large enough, it's a good idea to have three or four of these frozen tails stashed away against an emergency. Mashed or boiled potatoes,* and peas* or corn* are good accompaniments. Have the vegetables ready before you start the lobster.

☞ **HAVE ON HAND**

2 rock lobster tails	**lemon**
butter	**salt**
capers	**black peppercorns**
parsley	

Thaw the tails. With kitchen shears, cut off the soft belly shells, and discard them.

Loosen the meat from the top shell.

Preheat the oven to 475°. Melt ½ stick butter. Brush the empty top shell with butter and put the meat back in. Brush with butter, season with a little salt and pepper, and place, shell side down, in an iron skillet. Cook, over low heat, on top of the stove for 5 minutes. Brush again with butter and put the skillet under the broiler 4 inches from the heat. Broil for 3 minutes.

Add ½ teaspoon chopped parsley and 2 teaspoons drained capers to the remaining butter. Put the lobster tails on warm plates, pour the butter sauce over them, and garnish with lemon wedges.

When the Exchequer Is Low

*Every now and then we come face to face with the fact
that it's still two days until payday and there isn't much
money in the household purse. The following ten recipes
are designed to cope, in varying degrees, with "Operation
Emergency." In each case I'm leaving the desserts up to
you since I don't know exactly how low the exchequer is.*

BARBECUED LAMB RIBLETS
CARROTS* OR SPICY SQUASH CASSEROLE*

These are like little spareribs, only they come from
lamb instead of pork. They are absurdly inexpensive and
can be found, packaged, in most supermarkets. If you
can't find them that way, your butcher can cut them for
you.

☞ **HAVE ON HAND**
> 2 pounds lamb riblets
> salt, black peppercorns
> carrots or 1 package frozen squash
> butter
> parsley for carrots* or
> light brown sugar and ginger for squash*
> commercial barbecue sauce

Preheat the oven to 350°.

The riblets will take 1½ hours, so fix the vegetable while they are cooking. Wipe the ribs with paper towels and season them with salt and freshly ground black pepper. Put them in a shallow baking dish. Brush them with barbecue sauce and put them in the oven. Baste at 15-minute intervals with the sauce. Turn them occasionally so that they brown on all sides.

CASSEROLE OF LAMB RIBLETS AND GREEN BEANS
RICE* OR MASHED POTATOES*

No other vegetable is needed with this casserole. Take your choice of rice* or potatoes* to accompany it.

☞ **HAVE ON HAND**
> 1 pound lamb riblets
> onion
> medium-sized carrot
> ½ pound green beans
> salt, black peppercorns, rosemary
> vinegar (any kind)
> butter
> arrowroot flour or cornstarch (optional)

Wipe the riblets with paper towels and brown them in 1 tablespoon butter in a heavy skillet over moderate heat. Sprinkle with salt, freshly ground black pepper and a pinch of rosemary. Add enough cold water to cover, put a lid on the skillet, and simmer, over low heat, for 30 minutes.

Meanwhile, peel 1 small onion and chop it. Scrape and slice 1 medium-sized carrot. Wash the green beans and cut them crosswise. After the ribs have cooked 30 minutes, add the vegetables and continue to simmer another 30 minutes, until they are tender. Add 1 teaspoon vinegar 10 minutes before cooking time is up. If you like, you may thicken the sauce by adding 1 teaspoon arrowroot flour or cornstarch dissolved in a little cold water. Stir in and simmer for a few seconds.

**CUBED STEAKS
ZUCCHINI*
BAKED POTATOES***

These inexpensive steaks take only a couple of minutes to cook, so get everything else done before you put them in the pan.

☞ **HAVE ON HAND**
  2 cubed steaks, ½ pound each
  2 medium-sized zucchini
  butter
  Lawry's Seasoned Salt, salt, black peppercorns
  thyme, marjoram
  Parmesan cheese (¼ pound in one piece)
  2 Idaho potatoes
  lemon

Take the steaks out of the refrigerator as usual. Sprinkle
them with Lawry's Salt, freshly ground black pepper, and
pinches of thyme and marjoram.

Cook the zucchini, peeled and left whole, as in
Steamed Squash.* Cut it in half lengthwise before adding cheese and butter.

Cut 2 thin slices of lemon and put a tiny dab of butter
on each. Have ¼ of a stick of butter sizzling in a skillet
big enough to accommodate the steaks. Put the steaks
in the skillet and sauté over fairly high heat, turning
once, until brown on both sides. About 4 minutes on a
side is sufficient if you like them pink. Put the lemon
and butter on top of the steaks when you serve them.
These steaks do not need to rest.

SPAGHETTI AND MEAT BALLS SCARPELLINO
GREEN SALAD*
FRENCH OR ITALIAN BREAD
CHEESE

For two reasons this recipe is for four instead of two.
In the first place, in order to be any good, the sauce must
cook for quite a long time and therefore cannot be made
in a very small quantity. In the second place, it is sometimes necessary to feed a couple of friends even when
the budget is in dire straits. If you aren't having company,
cook half the amount of spaghetti and freeze half of the
sauce for another day. Incidentally, your use of this recipe
need not be limited to lean days. It is so good that it is
fit for company no matter what the condition of the

budget is. Serve a California red wine under those circum-
stances. This menu would even be suitable for a buffet
supper; triple or quadruple the recipe and have lots of
bread, salad, cheese and wine.

☞ HAVE ON HAND
    1½ pounds lean ground chuck (beef)
    1 large egg or 2 small eggs
    salt, black peppercorns, oregano, basil
    bread crumbs
    olive oil
    peanut oil
    butter
    garlic
    2 No. 2 cans Italian plum tomatoes
    small can tomato paste
    1 pound vermicelli spaghetti
    Parmesan cheese
    French or Italian bread
    salad greens
    your choice of cheese

As I said, the sauce must cook a long time — 2 hours,
in fact. It can, however, be made the day before.

Mix the meat with the unbeaten egg, or eggs, 1 tablespoon salt, a generous grinding of black pepper and ¾ cup
bread crumbs. Form into tight meat balls the size of
Ping-Pong balls.

Put ¼ cup olive oil and ¼ cup peanut oil in a sizable
heavy skillet and add 1 peeled clove of garlic. Turn on
the heat to moderate. When the garlic is sizzling but not
yet brown, fish it out. Add the meat balls and brown them
thoroughly on all sides. You have to stay with this, more
or less, but during the process you will be able to drain
the tomatoes, discarding the juice.

When the meat is brown, add the tomatoes, the tomato paste, 1 teaspoon salt, a grinding of black pepper and pinches of oregano and basil. Simmer slowly, over low heat, uncovered, for 2 hours. Stir every 10 minutes to prevent sticking and to coat the meat balls evenly. Just before mixing with spaghetti, add a tablespoon of butter.

Sometime during this process (if you are cooking on the day of the dinner), slice the loaf of bread slantwise down to within an ace of the bottom crust. Rub each slice with spit clove of garlic (unless you don't want to) and push soft butter down between each slice. Wrap the loaf in aluminum foil or the paper in which it came. Put it in a medium oven (350°) about 20 minutes before you serve dinner.

Again assuming that you are cooking on the day of the dinner, when the sauce is about done, fill your biggest pot with 4 quarts of water. Add 2 teaspoons salt and bring to a rolling boil. Add the spaghetti and cook 10 to 15 minutes, stirring frequently and watching all the time. After 8 minutes, fish out a piece and bite it. Do this again, once a minute thereafter. As soon as it does not taste actually raw, it is done. Put it in a large colander and run hot water from the tap over it for 2 (and only 2) minutes. Let it drain thoroughly and mix with the sauce. Have plenty of Parmesan cheese on hand, freshly grated.

RISOTTO
GREEN SALAD°

This is a good supper dish and should be remembered when you have chicken or turkey broth left over. It would be nice to follow this entrée with an interesting and "fruitful" dessert if the budget can be stretched to include it.

☞HAVE ON HAND
      enriched long-grain rice
      butter
      large yellow onion
      1¼ cups chicken or turkey broth, or half broth and half
         water
      salt, black peppercorns
      Parmesan cheese (¼ pound in one piece)

Put the broth in a saucepan on an asbestos pad over low heat.

Peel and chop the onion.

Melt 1 tablespoon butter in a deep saucepan over moderate heat. Add the onion and ½ cup rice. Stir until the rice is coated with butter and the onion is golden. Stir in the hot liquid. Add ½ teaspoon salt and a grinding of black pepper. Cover tightly and cook over low heat until all liquid is absorbed.

While the rice is cooking, grate enough Parmesan cheese to make 2 tablespoons.

Mix the rice and cheese together and serve hot.

MEAT LOAF
MASHED POTATOES*
GREEN BEANS*

This is not an ordinary meat loaf. It's fun to make and to eat. Any green vegetable would be as good with it as beans. It cooks for 1 hour, so you have plenty of time to fix the vegetable.

☞ **HAVE ON HAND**
> ¾ pound lean chuck (beef), ¼ pound lean veal and
> ½ pound lean pork ground together by the butcher
> white bread
> Worcestershire sauce
> salt, black peppercorns, marjoram
> egg
> small onion
> chili sauce
> condensed tomato soup
> small green pepper (optional)

Preheat the oven to 350°.

Take the meat out of the refrigerator as usual and put it in a bowl.

Sprinkle 1 slice crustless white bread with Worcestershire sauce and then hold the bread briefly under the cold-water faucet. Squeeze it out, over the sink, and then crumble it lightly into the meat. Add 1 teaspoon salt, a grinding of black pepper, a pinch of marjoram, 1 whole egg and 1 small peeled and grated onion. If you are fond of green peppers, add a small one, washed, seeded and chopped fine. Add 1 tablespoon chili sauce and mix lightly with your hands. Form into a loaf and place in a high-sided pan — a bread pan will do nicely. Pour ½ can tomato soup over the loaf and put it into the oven for 1 hour.

MACARONI AND CHEESE
GREEN SALAD*

This old but good stand-by can come in very handy if "Operation Emergency" is on and you are both hungry. A green vegetable could either take the place of salad or be added to the menu.

☞ **HAVE ON HAND**
>9-ounce package of macaroni
>hard cheese, rat-trap or Parmesan (¼ pound in one piece)
>butter
>milk
>salt, black peppercorns
>dry mustard
>bread crumbs
>flour

Preheat the oven to 350°.

Grate enough cheese to make ¼ cup. Butter a 6- or 7-inch casserole or baking dish.

Make 1 cup White Sauce.* Add a pinch of dry mustard.

Cook half the package of macaroni according to the instructions on the box. Drain it and mix it with 1 tablespoon butter. Melt 1 tablespoon butter in a small skillet and add to it ¼ cup bread crumbs. Brown briefly over low heat.

Put half the macaroni in the casserole. Sprinkle with half the cheese and cover with half the sauce. Add the rest of the macaroni and repeat. Top with the buttered crumbs and bake until brown and bubbly. If you are very fond of cheese, you may use much more. The dish may also be made with leftover cooked rice.

HAMBURGERS

The secret of making good hamburgers is to handle the meat as little as possible. Here are the two ways of cooking them, whether you are going to put them in buns or whether you are going to build a meal around them. Canned or frozen French fried onion rings go well with hamburgers, as do stewed tomatoes.* Another idea is to top each hamburger with a fried egg.*

☞ **HAVE ON HAND**
    1 pound lean round steak or chuck (beef)
    butter
    Lawry's Seasoned Salt, salt, black peppercorns

Divide the meat into 2 or 4 portions. Lightly shape each into a round, slightly flat cake about an inch or more thick. To sauté, have 1 scant tablespoon butter sizzling in a skillet. Put the hamburgers in and cook them over a little better than moderate heat for 5 to 6 minutes on each side for rare meat and a little longer for better-done. Turn them only once and don't poke at them. Season with Lawry's Salt and pepper before serving.

To grill them, have the broiler hot and see that the meat is about 2 inches from the heat. Cook for 6 minutes on each side or a little more for better-done meat. Season as above.

Most men have their own ideas about hamburgers. If your husband likes to add Worcestershire sauce, red wine, onions or herbs, let him.

Leftovers

Here are a few ways to make interesting and appetizing
hot and cold dishes out of leftover meat and poultry.

LAMB MOLD
GREEN OR WHITE ASPARAGUS VINAIGRETTE*
CHOCOLATE SOUFFLÉ*

If you have enough leftover lamb to make a cupful,
have this pleasant cold supper and top it off with a
soufflé. The mold has to chill for a long time, so you
might as well make it the day before and leave yourself
free for dessert-making on the day of the dinner.

☞ **HAVE ON HAND**
  cold lamb
  unflavored gelatin
  tomato juice
  salt, marjoram
  lemon
  prepared mustard
  onion
  stalk celery
  pimiento
  mayonnaise
  1 box frozen asparagus or 1 can white asparagus
  French dressing*
  lettuce leaves
  parsley
  chives
  cucumber pickle
  capers (optional)

Cut enough lamb into cubes (about the size of dice) to make 1 cup.

Soften 1 envelope of gelatin in ¼ cup cold water in a small bowl.

Put ¾ cup tomato juice, a dash of salt and a pinch of marjoram in a saucepan and bring to a boil. Pour the juice over the gelatin and stir. When the gelatin has dissolved, add 1 tablespoon lemon juice and 1 teaspoon mustard. Mix well. Put in refrigerator.

Mix 1 teaspoon grated onion, ¼ cup chopped celery, 1 tablespoon chopped pimiento and ¼ cup mayonnaise with the lamb. Look at the gelatin mixture and see if it has begun to thicken. When it has, fold the lamb into it.

Rinse a 1-quart casserole with cold water. Spoon the mixture into the casserole and chill until firm.

To remove from the mold, run a sharp knife around

the inside edge of the casserole. Let the casserole stand for a minute or two in hot water. Put a cold plate or small round platter over the casserole and turn the whole business upside down. Serve on lettuce leaves with extra mayonnaise on the side.

> ### BARBECUED LAMB HASH
> ### GREEN BEANS*
> ### BROWN BETTY*

If you have the same amount of lamb left over but the weather is chilly and you'd rather have it hot, try this. The Brown Betty* will take 45 minutes to bake, so put it in the oven before you start the hash or the beans. Everything will be ready at the same time.

☞ **HAVE ON HAND**
> leftover lamb
> small onion
> butter
> barbecue sauce
> large Irish potato
> ½ pound green beans or 1 box frozen
> salt, black peppercorns

Peel the potato and put it in a saucepan with enough boiling water to cover and simmer 20 minutes or until just tender. Drain it and cut it into cubes.

Meanwhile, cube the lamb as in the preceding recipe. In a sizable skillet, sauté 1 small chopped onion in 1 tablespoon butter until golden. Add the lamb and brown it over moderate heat. Add 1 cup barbecue sauce and simmer, covered, over low heat for 15 minutes. Add the cubed potatoes to the hash and allow to heat for 10 minutes. Season to taste with salt and freshly ground black pepper.

MIROTON OF BEEF
RICE°
FRIED EGGPLANT°
HOT FRUIT COMPOTE°

This is a French way to cope with your leftover roast beef. The whole thing takes about half an hour.

☞ **HAVE ON HAND**

3 or 4 thin slices cold roast beef	bouillon cube
¼ pound mushrooms	tomato catsup
butter	parsley
medium-sized onion	rice
cider vinegar	small eggplant
flour	peanut oil
salt, black peppercorns, thyme	bread crumbs

Trim the fat from the slices of beef and cut each slice into matchlike strips. You should have a heaping cupful of slivers.

Wash, dry, and slice ¼ pound mushrooms and cook them, over moderate heat, in 1 tablespoon butter for 5 minutes or until lightly browned. Remove the mushrooms with a slotted spoon and add ¼ cup chopped onion to the pan. Add a little more butter if necessary and cook until

━✽━◉━✽━◉━✽━◉━✽━◉━✽━◉━✽━◉━✽━◉━✽━◉━✽━◉━✽━◉━✽━

the onion is lightly browned. Add ½ teaspoon cider vinegar. Mix in 1 teaspoon flour and a pinch of powdered
thyme. Stir well.

Dissolve ½ bouillon cube in ½ cup boiling water and
add it to the onion mixture slowly. Stir. When the sauce
is thick, add ½ tablespoon tomato catsup, a dash of salt,
a grinding of black pepper, ½ tablespoon chopped parsley
and the mushrooms. Simmer 2 minutes. Add the beef,
cover, and simmer 5 minutes. Keep this warm on an asbestos pad over low heat while you cook the rice* and fry
the eggplant.*

> **BEEF SALAD FERMIÈRE**
> **HOT FRENCH BREAD**
> **CHEESE AND FRUIT**

We are still cooking with a French accent. This is a
hearty peasant dish and should be accompanied by the
things which would be served with it in a French farm-
house: bread, cheese, fruit and of course some inexpensive
red wine.

☞ **HAVE ON HAND**
    ½ pound leftover beef, roasted or boiled
    1 slice fat salt pork
    beef bouillon cube
    rice
    tomato

small onion
parsley
chervil, salt, black peppercorns
dry mustard
eggs
peanut or olive oil
tarragon vinegar

Cook, by the directions on the box, enough rice to make 1 cup; usually this is about ½ cup raw rice. You may use precooked rice for this dish, incidentally.

Remove the rind from the piece of salt pork. This is a hard strip along one side. Dice the salt pork and sauté it in a small skillet over moderate heat until crisp and lightly browned. This is called, of all things, "trying out." Remove the bits of salt pork with a slotted spoon and drain them on paper towels. The clear fat left from the "trying out" may go into your storage can for cooking fat.

Dissolve ½ beef bouillon cube in ¼ cup boiling water.

Make ¼ cup Vinaigrette sauce by mixing together 1 tablespoon tarragon vinegar, 3 tablespoons oil with salt, freshly ground black pepper and dry mustard to taste. Mix this sauce with the broth you made from the bouillon cube.

Cut the beef into very thin slices and mix it with the rice, salt pork, 1 small onion (minced), 1 tablespoon chopped parsley, a pinch of chervil, ⅛ teaspoon salt and a grinding of black pepper. Mix with the sauce and chill. This may be done the day before.

In the morning of the day you're having the salad, hard-boil 2 eggs.* Peel 1 tomato,* seed it, slice it thinly, and chill it.

Serve the salad garnished with the tomato slices and quartered hard-boiled eggs.

SALMI OF DUCK
PEAS*
RICE* OR NOODLES*
CODDLING CREAM*

A "salmi" is a ragout or stew made of roasted game or duck. It is such a good dish that it is often made out of pheasant, partridge or duck roasted particularly for the purpose. In this case we are using leftover duck, and I believe you'll agree with me that it is a stew worthy of its fancy name. Peas and duck are practically inseparable; take your choice of rice* or noodles,* and by all means have an apple dessert, whether it is this one, Apples Bonne Femme* or Apple Pie.*

☞ HAVE ON HAND
    a duck carcass with a fair amount of meat on it
    duck liver
    chicken bouillon cube
    butter
    dry red wine
    peanut or olive oil
    salt, black peppercorns
    lemon
    small jar pitted green olives
    arrowroot flour or cornstarch
    1 package frozen peas or 1 pound fresh

Pick off all the meat from the duck carcass and put it aside.

Dissolve ½ chicken bouillon cube in ¼ cup boiling water. Wash the duck liver and simmer it in this broth, over medium heat, until it is soft. Mash it in the broth, using a fork. When it is a paste, put it in a larger saucepan with 1 tablespoon butter, ½ cup red wine, 1 tablespoon peanut or olive oil, a dash of salt, a grinding of black pepper and ½ teaspoon grated lemon peel. Simmer, over very low heat, covered, for 30 minutes. Add the pieces of duck, cutting up any large ones. Bring back to simmer. Add 1 scant teaspoon cornstarch or arrowroot flour softened in ¼ cup water. Stir and simmer until thick. Add ½ cup sliced or whole pitted olives. Boil the rice* or noodles* and cook the peas* while the sauce is simmering or after the salmi is all ready and keeping warm.

HAM CURRY
VEGETABLE SALAD*
CHILLED FRUIT COMPOTE*

I found this recipe in a yellowed newspaper clipping pasted in my grandmother's notebook. I've never encountered it in a modern cookbook, but it's very good. I have used it instead of some form of eggs at Sunday brunch and for a light supper with the accompaniments listed above. For the salad, look up Vegetable Salad* and cut the recipe down to the amount you need.

☞ **HAVE ON HAND**
   enough chopped leftover ham to make 1 cup
   small onion
   white bread
   milk
   butter
   eggs
   curry powder, salt

Preheat the oven to 250°.

Melt 1 teaspoon butter in a small skillet and sauté half a small onion, peeled and minced, until brown. Have the heat moderate. Add 1 slice crustless white bread and ½ cup milk. Allow to stand, away from the heat, for 10 minutes or more.

Separate 2 eggs.* Beat the yolks lightly with a fork and add them to the bread in the skillet with the ham and 1 teaspoon curry powder. Mix with a fork.

Butter a 7-inch casserole or baking dish.

Beat the egg whites, with a pinch of salt, until stiff but not dry. Dump the egg, ham and bread mixture over them and fold in. Spoon it into the casserole and bake for 30 minutes.

> **CURRY**
> **RICE°**
> **CHUTNEY**
> **GREEN BEANS°**
> **ORANGE° OR LIME ICE**

Leftover lamb or chicken, hard-boiled eggs, cooked shrimp, lobster or crabmeat may be heated in this quick and easy curry sauce. Curry, which should always be served with fluffy rice,* may be accompanied solely by chutney or by a group of side dishes containing such things as grated coconut, chopped peanuts, chopped hard-boiled eggs, chopped crisp bacon and minced onions. Take your choice of any or all of these. Beer is to curry what champagne is to lobster; have some.

☞ **HAVE ON HAND**
  butter
  small onion
  curry powder
  arrowroot flour or cornstarch
  1 package frozen green beans or ½ pound fresh
  salt, black peppercorns
  root ginger
  brown sugar
  leftover meat, fish, or eggs

Melt 1 tablespoon butter and sauté in it, over moderate heat, 1 small onion, peeled and minced, and a small piece of root ginger.

Mix 1 scant tablespoon arrowroot flour or cornstarch, 1 teaspoon curry powder, ½ teaspoon brown sugar, ⅛ teaspoon salt and a grinding of black pepper. Stir this into the butter and onion. Lower the heat slightly. When blended, add 1 cup warm milk. Simmer and stir until thick and smooth.

If you are using leftover chicken, remove the meat

from the bones, cut it into bite-sized pieces, and heat it in the sauce. If lamb is your ingredient, cut it also in bite-sized pieces, remove all fat, and heat it in the sauce. Shrimp are heated peeled but whole, lobster cut up, and crab meat used in lumps from which all bits of cartilage have been carefully removed. Eggs are sliced.

This amount of sauce will take care of 1 cup of any of the above. Double or triple the recipe if you have more leftovers. Whatever you don't eat may be frozen. Curry may also be made the day before; as a matter of fact, it is even better that way.

CROQUETTES

Croquettes provide an excellent answer to the problem of leftover poultry or meat. They can be made ahead of time; in fact they must be, to a certain extent, since they have to be chilled before they are cooked. If you have enough leftovers, you should make more than you will need for one meal, since they freeze well. Cook them all, cool the ones you're not using, wrap in freezer paper, label, and freeze. When you want to serve these extra ones, heat them in butter. This recipe will make 4 to 6 croquettes, depending on how big you make them. Beef or veal croquettes may be served with canned or bottled tomato sauce which you have seasoned to taste; chicken, turkey or ham croquettes should have a White Sauce* to which you have added a touch of lemon juice and a grinding of nutmeg. Any croquettes may be served with gravy left over from the main ingredient. Peas are the classic accompaniment for croquettes, but other green vegetables are equally good, I find.

☞ **HAVE ON HAND**
    flour
    butter
    milk, cream or half-and-half
    chicken or turkey broth (for poultry croquettes)
    enough leftovers to make 2 cups of minced solids
    small onion
    parsley
    salt, black peppercorns
    cayenne pepper, celery salt
    eggs
    lemon (for chicken or turkey croquettes)
    chili sauce (for beef croquettes)
    peanut oil
    bread crumbs

Make a white sauce which is thicker than usual by melting 2 tablespoons butter, stirring in 3 tablespoons flour, and slowly adding 1 cup scalded milk,* cream or half-and-half; or half chicken or turkey broth and half milk, cream, etc.

Put cold cooked chicken, turkey, steak, roast beef, veal or ham through the meat grinder with 1 small peeled onion and 2 or 3 sprigs parsley. Add salt and freshly ground black pepper to taste. You must have 2 cups of meat or poultry. Add this to the cream sauce, away from the heat. Beat 1 whole egg and stir it in. Put back on moderate heat and cook and stir 1 minute. Season to taste with salt, celery salt, and cayenne pepper. Add lemon juice if the ingredient is poultry, 1 tablespoon chili sauce if it is beef. Spread the mixture in a buttered pan and allow to cool slightly.

Have ready 1 egg diluted with ¼ cup milk and 1 tablespoon peanut oil. Add ¼ teaspoon salt. Also have 1 inch of bread crumbs on a platter.

Shape the croquettes into cones, cylinders or balls. Roll each croquette in the egg mixture so that it is completely coated. Allow surplus liquid to drain off. There must be just enough moisture to hold the crumbs. Then roll the croquettes in the crumbs, being careful that all surfaces are covered. When all the croquettes are crumbed, chill them for 3 hours or overnight.

Fry them in deep hot fat (390°) until golden brown on all sides, or sauté them in a mixture of melted butter and peanut oil. In the latter case, have about an inch of oil and butter in the skillet and sauté the croquettes one or two at a time. Whether fried or sautéed, drain them on paper towels as they become done.

Vegetables

HOW TO SHOP FOR VEGETABLES

First of all, don't buy vegetables, or fruits either, for that matter, which are wrapped in cellophane or put up in bags. Unfortunately, not everyone is honest and many a housewife has brought home a handsome, cellophane-covered box of asparagus only to find that several stalks at the bottom have to be thrown away. Even in supermarkets, where so many items are packaged, you can find vegetables and fruits which are not. These are the ones to choose from.

Buy fresh vegetables when they are in season in your vicinity. They will have come from nearby farms and will be fresher and less expensive than if they have had to travel from some other part of the country where they are in season. What's more, they won't be from a hothouse. When you feel that you must have something which is out of season, buy frozen foods or some of the fine canned vegetables. While our canning is not quite up to that of the French, there are exceptions, notably shoe-peg and whole-kernel corn, tomatoes, artichoke bottoms and some brands of white asparagus. The French do better than we do with tiny peas and small whole green beans, which can be found at most grocers and are not expensive.

When you are shopping for fresh vegetables, look for artichokes which are heavy and green with close-set, fleshy leaves; asparagus with tightly closed tips and green stalks; slender, smooth green or wax beans which snap easily; firm creamy-white cauliflower with bright green leaves; slender carrots; corn with the husks still on; dark green broccoli without opened buds; crisp green Brussels sprouts; celery with fresh leaves and no rust spots; small firm eggplants. Mushrooms should be white-skinned and firm. Onions should have brittle skins; your taste, or the recipe in which you are going to use them, determines whether they should be Bermuda (sweet), yellow, white, red or green. Don't buy potatoes that are sprouting. Here again, the type to buy depends on how you're going to cook them; your choices are sweet potatoes or yams, Idaho potatoes for baking, old potatoes for mashing, and Irish potatoes or new potatoes for boiling. As for squash, I think that you'll be using frozen squash for the most part, but you will buy zucchini, I hope. This should be small to medium, dark green and crisp. Tomatoes should be deep red, green or streaked — not pink because those are hothouse.

With the exception of potatoes and onions, vegetables should be washed at once and stored in the crisper compartment of your refrigerator.

ARTICHOKES (1 per person)

Pull off all dreary-looking lower leaves and cut the stems flush with the bottoms of the artichokes. With kitchen shears, cut off the prickly tips of the leaves. Soak the artichokes in cold water for a half hour or so.

Have enough salted water boiling in a deep saucepan to cover the artichokes. The water doesn't actually cover them, because they float; but have considerable water anyway. Add 1 teaspoon salt and the juice of half a lemon. Boil them, uncovered, until a bottom leaf may be easily detached. Detach it and nibble it. If it is as tender as you like it, the artichokes are done. (Some people like them firm, some mushy.) Cooking time will be between 30 and 50 minutes, depending on the size of the artichokes. Test after 30 minutes. When they are done, drain them upside down so that all water runs out. Serve hot with melted butter or Hollandaise Sauce,* or cold with French* or Vinaigrette* Dressing. Frozen artichokes, cooked by the directions on the box, are good served hot with sauce or cold in a salad.

ASPARAGUS (1 pound fresh, 1 box frozen or 1 No. 2 can serves 2)

Canned white asparagus is very good, but I cannot say the same for the green. If you yearn for green asparagus when it is out of season, use the frozen; get "jumbo" spears.

To cook fresh asparagus, break off the tough ends and trim the stalks with a knife so that they are all of uniform length. The reason for breaking the stalks is that the break will occur just at the juncture between the tough and tender parts. Wash the asparagus and scrape the bottom

2 inches of the stalk. Tie two strings around the stalks, one towards the top of the bunch and one towards the bottom.

Have enough water boiling in a deep saucepan to cover the asparagus or have 2 inches in the bottom of an asparagus cooker. Add **1 teaspoon salt.** Cover an asparagus cooker, but do not cover a saucepan. Boil the asparagus until it is tender but still slightly crisp. Test the lower part of the stalks after 20 minutes. Slender stalks will take less time than thick ones. Drain them thoroughly and keep them warm. The tray in an asparagus cooker may be lifted out with the asparagus on it, and, with a long-handled wooden spoon through the handles, it will hold the asparagus out of the water. Have the water simmering and cover the asparagus with aluminum foil. Serve asparagus with **melted butter, browned butter,*** or **Hollandaise Sauce.*** Two tablespoons **bread crumbs** may be browned in the butter, making the dish "Asparagus Polonaise."

Asparagus may be cooked by the cold-water method, which I like. Put it in enough cold water to cover, add the salt, and test after it has come to a boil and has simmered for 10 minutes. The only difficulty is that you must watch it like a hawk and time it from the minute it boils; otherwise, it may get overdone and be limp.

Treat frozen or canned asparagus the same as fresh as far as sauce is concerned. Any cooked asparagus is good cold, with French* or Vinaigrette* Dressing.

GREEN OR WAX BEANS (½ *pound fresh or 1 box frozen serves 2*)

The best frozen beans are tiny whole ones, if you can find them. As a matter of fact, so are the best fresh ones.

If you can't get fresh ones like that, get the slenderest ones you can. Wash them and snap off both ends. Cut them crosswise or "French" them by cutting them in slanting slices. Cook in just enough boiling salted water (**1 teaspoon salt**) to cover. Eat one piece after 15 minutes. If it is crisply tender, drain the beans thoroughly and keep them warm in a colander over simmering water. When ready to serve, douse them with **2 tablespoons butter** which you have allowed to get golden brown. **Three or four mushrooms** may be washed, dried, sliced, sautéed in the butter, and added to the beans; or you may sauté and add **2 tablespoons of slivered almonds.**

LIMA BEANS (1 pound fresh or 1 box frozen serves 2)

Frozen limas are good because only very young and tender beans are selected for freezing. Try to find fresh ones in smallish pods; buy them in the pods. Shell them yourself just before cooking and proceed as in green beans. Drain thoroughly and serve with **melted butter.** For succotash, mix the beans with an equal amount of cooked **corn,** * scraped from the cob, butter and a little cream. Frozen corn or canned whole-kernel corn may also be used.

BEETS (½ pound fresh or 1 No. 2 can serves 2)

Now here is one situation when the canned product is almost as good as the fresh and ever so much simpler to prepare. Fresh beets seem to be so odd about boiling, for one thing; they boil over without warning, and when you turn down the heat to the point where you feel they should be simmering, they stop boiling altogether. And they bleed so. Even when you leave the root and a good

2 inches of top on them, your sink looks like an abattoir when you drain them. *And* they dirty the pot so. However, if you really want to cook fresh beets, here's how. Trim them as above and scrub them. (If the greens are nice-looking, young and fresh, wash them, put them in the crisper, and cook them, in the water which clings to them, for another meal. Season them with **salt, pepper** and **lemon juice.**) To go back to the beets, cook them in boiling salted water (1 teaspoon salt) to cover for 30 minutes to an hour, depending on the size of the beets. Drain, peel, and cut them in dice or slices.

From now on, the procedure is the same for fresh or drained canned beets. Heat them in **1 generous tablespoon butter** and season to taste with **salt, freshly ground black pepper** and a **pinch of tarragon or marjoram.**

BROCCOLI (*1 pound fresh or 1 box frozen serves 2*)

Soak fresh broccoli in cold water for a half hour. Drain and discard all wilted or tough outer leaves. Cut off the tough part of the stem. Cut the rest of the stem in 1-inch slices. Have sufficient water boiling to cover the broccoli. Add **1 teaspoon salt** and the stem slices. Cook 5 minutes and add the rest of the broccoli. Cook for about 10 minutes, until the stem slices are tender. Drain thoroughly and serve with **melted butter, browned butter*** with or without **bread crumbs,** Hollandaise Sauce* or bake it as in Cauliflower au Gratin.*

Frozen broccoli is excellent. Cook it according to directions on the box and treat it in any of the ways mentioned above.

BRUSSELS SPROUTS (1 pint fresh or 1 box frozen serves 2)

There's practically no difference in taste between fresh and frozen Brussels sprouts. Fresh sprouts must be soaked in cold water and very carefully picked over. Outer leaves must be discarded, tips of the stems cut off and wormy places ferreted out and removed. You might as well stick to the frozen. Once fresh sprouts have been coped with as above, they are cooked exactly as frozen ones are, only a touch longer. Both are put into boiling salted water and boiled briskly. The frozen ones take about 10 minutes, fresh between 15 and 20. Neither kind should be overcooked and both should be very thoroughly drained; in fact, it's a good idea to put them in a colander, set the colander over the pan in which the sprouts were cooked, and let them stay there for a bit.

Meanwhile, melt **1 tablespoon butter** in a small casserole over low heat. Add the **Brussels sprouts,** a **grinding of black pepper** and one of **nutmeg** (most important) and **¼ cup light cream.** Toss with a fork. The sprouts may be kept warm, on an asbestos pad over low heat. Repeat the tossing with a fork occasionally.

CABBAGE

Even a small young cabbage is apt to be too much for two people. Cook half of it and make Coleslaw* with the rest.

Take off the outer leaves and cut the part that you are going to use in half. Soak it in cold water for 15 minutes or so. Have a good deal of water boiling in a deep saucepan. Add **1 teaspoon salt.** Separate the leaves of the cabbage and drop them, one by one, into the water. Cook for 5 minutes. A **piece of bread** placed on top of the boiling cabbage will keep it from advertising its presence throughout the house. Drain the cabbage (need I say thoroughly?) and toss it, in a heated serving dish, with **1 tablespoon melted butter, salt to taste** and a **grinding of black pepper.**

CARROTS

Carrots will keep for a long time in the crisper compartment of the refrigerator. Buy a bunch of small ones and, for buttered carrots, use 3 or 4 for each person. Cut a little off the end of each carrot. If the carrots are very young and smooth, they need only to be scrubbed. Older ones should be scraped with a knife or peeled with a vegetable peeler. Leave tiny young carrots whole; slice older ones, dice them, or cut them into slivers. Have enough water boiling to barely cover them. Add **1 teaspoon salt** and cook the carrots for 10 to 20 minutes, until tender but not mushy. Drain and heat in **1 tablespoon butter.** Add salt to taste and a **grinding of black pepper.** Chopped **parsley or mint** may be sprinkled on top. Diced cooked carrots may be mixed with an equal amount of cooked **peas.**

Carrots are very good mashed. You will need a whole bunch for two servings. Scrub or scrape them, cut them into chunks, and boil them as above until really soft. Drain them and put them through a ricer. Mash them with a potato masher or a wooden spoon, adding as you do so 1 generous tablespoon butter and ¼ **cup light cream.** Season to taste with salt and freshly ground black pepper. Keep warm indefinitely on an asbestos pad over low heat.

CAULIFLOWER AU GRATIN (1 small head serves 2)

I think that the way you two probably like cauliflower best is "au gratin." If I am wrong, or if you don't want to go to the trouble of making white sauce, just cook it as described below and serve it Polonaise, with **browned butter** and **bread crumbs.**

Remove the larger leaves and cut the stalk flush with the bottom of the cauliflower. Separate the cauliflower into flowerets. If you were unable to get a really small head, put a few flowerets into the crisper compartment and save them to serve raw with cocktails. Soak the number of flowerets you need in cold water for a few minutes. Meanwhile put enough water to cover them in a saucepan, bring it to a boil, add 1 teaspoon salt and the drained cauliflower. Cook until just tender, about 12 to 15 minutes. Drain them and let them sit in a colander while you make the white sauce.

Put **1 cup half-and-half, light cream or milk** in a measuring cup or saucepan. Set it on an asbestos pad over low heat. Turn on the oven to 450°.

Melt **1 tablespoon butter** in a heavy saucepan and stir in **1 scant tablespoon flour.** Cook over low heat, stirring with a wooden spoon, until smooth. Add the hot liquid gradually, stirring constantly. Add **½ teaspoon Worcestershire sauce,** a **pinch of white pepper** and **salt** to taste. Put the **drained cauliflower** in a casserole just big enough to hold it. Pour in the sauce.

Grate **½ cup Parmesan cheese.** Sprinkle this and **¼ cup bread crumbs** over the cauliflower. Heat in the oven for about 15 minutes or until brown and bubbly.

Boiled cauliflower may also be served with Hollandaise.*

CORN (*the number of ears depends on you*)

Corn is much tenderer when cooked by the cold-water method. After husking it and removing all the silk, put it in enough cold water to cover, add 1 teaspoon salt, and bring to a boil, uncovered. Start timing when the water really boils. Young corn will take no more than 5 minutes; older corn will take 10. Do not overcook.

To scrape corn, slit the kernels by drawing a sharp knife down the middle of each row. Scrape onto a plate, using the dull edge of the knife.

CELERY (*1 pound serves 2*)

Buy a 1-pound bunch of Pascal celery. Wash it thoroughly. Cut off the leafy tops and save them to add to boiling meat or fowl, or to put inside a duck. Save any tough outer stalks for the same purpose. Save the heart to eat at the table.

Cut the rest of the celery into 1-inch pieces. Cook in just enough boiling, lightly salted water to cover for 10 to 15 minutes. Watch carefully to see that the celery doesn't burn. Drain it and reserve the water.

Make 1 cup White Sauce* using, for the liquid, half celery stock and half milk or cream. Taste before seasoning with salt. Mix the sauce with the celery and keep it warm in the usual way.

EGGPLANT (*¾ pound serves 2*)

Wash a **small eggplant.** Do not peel it. Cut it into slices about ¼ inch thick. Dry with paper towels. Turn on the oven to 300°.

Put **1 inch of bread crumbs** on a platter. Put 2 thicknesses of paper towels on a cookie tin. Put **2 tablespoons** butter and ½ cup peanut oil in a skillet. Heat until the butter melts. You should have a little more than ¼ inch of fat. If you haven't that much, add a little more oil. Heat until it sizzles. Dip the slices of eggplant in the crumbs and sauté them, a few at a time, in the hot fat. When they are golden brown on both sides, they are done; take them out, put them on the paper-covered cookie sheet, and keep them warm in the oven.

ONIONS (½ pound or 1 medium-sized jar or can serves 2)

Small boiled white onions come in glass jars or cans. Heat them in their juice, drain, and serve with melted butter or White Sauce.*

French fried onions come frozen or in cans. Heat in the oven according to instructions on the box or can.

Buy yellow onions for occasions when the recipe reads, "sauté 1 medium onion," or "add 1 medium onion." Buy 1 pound at a time.

For boiled onions, buy ½ pound of white onions (silverskins). To peel any onion, hold it under cold running water while doing so. Or you may cover the onions with boiling water, let them stand for a minute with the heat turned off, drain them, and slip off the skins. After handling onions or garlic, wash your hands in cold water.

Cook silverskins, in enough boiling salted water to cover, for 20 minutes or until tender. If they are very small, they will take less time. Drain thoroughly and serve with melted butter and freshly ground black pepper or with White Sauce.*

For smothered onions to go with liver or steak, peel and slice thinly 2 medium-sized yellow onions. Sauté in

2 tablespoons butter over very low heat, turning often with a fork. Sprinkle with salt.

PEAS (*1 pound fresh, 1 box frozen or 1 No. 2 can serves 2*)

Do not shell fresh peas until you are about to cook them. Put them in enough boiling water to cover, and add 1 teaspoon salt. Lower the heat and simmer uncovered until just tender. Fish out one of the bigger peas and taste it after about 15 minutes. Drain and season with freshly ground black pepper, a pinch of sugar and a grinding of nutmeg. Toss with 1 tablespoon melted butter.

Frozen peas are good, especially the extra small ones. After cooking them according to the directions on the package, treat them as above.

PEAS AND MUSHROOMS

Cook fresh or frozen peas. Save the cooking liquid.

Wash but do not peel ¼ pound mushrooms. Cut off the tip of the stem and slice thinly. Sauté the mushrooms in 2 tablespoons butter over moderate heat until tender. Remove them temporarily to a plate. Add 1 tablespoon flour to the butter in the pan. Stir and cook.

Mix ¼ cup cream or half-and-half and ¼ cup juice from the peas. Stir this into the butter and flour. Add the peas and mushrooms; season to taste with salt and freshly ground black pepper. Simmer, covered, for a few minutes.

PEAS À LA FRANÇAISE

The only canned peas worth their salt, to my mind, are the No. 1 Sift Early June Peas. That's the way they are labeled and this is what you do with them. Put 1 tablespoon butter in a casserole. Add 2 or 3 leaves of lettuce (shredded), 4 small white onions (peeled), and the can of peas (drained). Add a pinch of sugar, a scant teaspoon salt, and grindings of black pepper and nutmeg. Cover and cook, over low heat, until the onions are tender. They can wait, on an asbestos pad, over low heat.

POTATOES ANNA

Preheat the oven to 450°.

Peel and slice extra thin 2 medium-sized Irish potatoes. Soak in ice water for a half hour. Melt 2 tablespoons butter. Drain and dry potatoes. Butter a small casserole and put a layer of potatoes in it. Dribble a little of the butter over them. Put in another layer and dribble more butter, and continue till all the potatoes are in. Dribble the remaining butter and put the casserole in the oven for 40 minutes or until potatoes are soft. Turn out on a warm serving dish and sprinkle with chopped parsley.

MASHED POTATOES

Peel 2 medium-sized old potatoes. Cut into quarters and soak in cold water for a half hour. Drain and cook, uncovered, in 2 cups boiling salted water. When they are soft, drain them thoroughly and put them through the ricer or mash them with a fork. Use the same pan in which they boiled, having kept it warm. Add 1 tablespoon hot cream, 1 generous tablespoon butter, salt and pepper to taste. Mash with a potato masher until smooth. Keep hot over boiling water, uncovered. If you have an electric mixer, put the drained potatoes, cream, butter and seasonings in the bowl and beat. Incidentally, try instant mashed potatoes. They are O.K.

BAKED POTATOES

Scrub **2 Idaho potatoes**, dry them and rub them with **bacon fat, peanut oil or butter** if you like crisp skins. Place them on the rack in a preheated 350° oven and bake for 40 minutes to an hour. After 30 minutes, prick them deeply with a fork in several places. This allows the steam to escape and prevents the potatoes from exploding, which, should it happen, is no fun. Test for doneness by squeezing one gently, while holding it in a towel. If the potato feels soft, it is done. Cut a gash in the top to let the steam escape and put a generous dab of butter in the opening. If you like, cut the potatoes in half lengthwise and scoop them out. Mash with **butter, salt, pepper and 1 teaspoon hot milk** per potato. Refill the skins, brush with butter and brown under the broiler.

PARSLEY POTATOES (½ pound serves 2)

Scrub **new potatoes** and cook them, uncovered, in boiling water to which you have added **1 teaspoon salt.** If they are small, they will take 12 to 15 minutes or longer. Test with a fork to see if they are done. Drain them, put them back in the pan, and shake them, over moderate heat, to dry. Wrap the potatoes in a kitchen towel and keep them hot until ready to serve. When the time comes, put them in a warm serving dish and pour over them **2 tablespoons melted butter.** Dust with **chopped parsley.** New potatoes in their skins are also good served with **sour cream** mixed with **chopped chives.**

If you wish, you may scrape the potatoes before cooking them. In that case, serve them with melted butter, chopped parsley and **1 tablespoon strained lemon juice.**

SCALLOPED POTATOES

Preheat the oven to 300°.

Pare **2 medium-sized Irish potatoes** and cut them in thin slices.

Butter a 6- or 7-inch casserole or baking dish and put in it a layer of potatoes. Sprinkle with **salt** and **pepper** and dot with **butter**. Repeat layers until all potato slices have been used. Add **milk** to just barely cover the top layer. Dot with butter, sprinkle with **paprika** and bake 1 hour.

HASHED BROWN POTATOES

Sometime before you want to hash them, wash **2 medium-sized Irish potatoes.** Have enough water boiling to cover them. Add **½ teaspoon salt** and the potatoes and simmer for 15 to 20 minutes, covered, until the potatoes are tender. Drain and cool.

Half an hour before dinner, slip off the skins and cut the potatoes into small dice. Mince enough **onion** to make 1 teaspoon and add this, with a **grinding of black pepper,** to the potatoes. Taste to see if more salt is necessary. Toss with a fork.

In a medium-sized skillet, melt **2 tablespoons butter** or 1 tablespoon butter with 1 tablespoon bacon drippings over low heat. Add the potatoes and press them down with a spatula. With the same spatula, pull them away from the sides of the skillet. Cook gently for 15 minutes. Fold them like an omelet and slip them onto a warm serving plate or turn them upside down onto the plate. If desired, **¼ cup hot cream** may be added to the potatoes just before they are done.

POTATOES BOULANGÈRE

These potatoes may be fixed ahead of time, all but a final 15 minutes of baking. This must be done in a 350° oven, so don't plan to have them if your oven must be hotter for some reason.

Scrub **2 medium-sized Irish potatoes** and cook as in the previous recipe. Drain, cool, and slice.

Peel and slice **1 medium-sized yellow onion.**

Dissolve **1 beef bouillon cube or ½ teaspoon beef extract** in ¼ cup boiling water.

Butter a small casserole, about 10 inches in diameter, and put in it a layer of potatoes, a layer of **Swiss cheese** (4 thin slices in all) and a layer of onions. Repeat until everything is in. Press down with the spatula.

Sprinkle with **bread crumbs,** pour the broth over all and dot with **butter,** liberally. If you have done all this long ahead of time, put the casserole in the refrigerator, but be sure to take it out an hour before baking so that it can warm up to room temperature. Bake for 15 minutes in a preheated 350° oven.

SWEET POTATOES

These are best mashed or candied. In either case they are first boiled. Wash **2 large sweet potatoes or yams.** Have enough water boiling to cover them. Add **½ teaspoon salt** and the potatoes and simmer them, covered, until softly tender for mashed potatoes and until just barely tender for candied potatoes. This will take between 20 and 30 minutes.

Peel off skins. For mashed sweet potatoes, mash them with a potato masher or a fork, adding **1 tablespoon or more soft butter** and **salt and pepper** to taste.

To candy them, peel and cut them into ½-inch slices crosswise. Have ⅓ **cup brown sugar** handy and **3 tablespoons butter.** Arrange the **sweet potatoes** in layers in a small, buttered casserole (10 inches) sprinkling each layer with sugar and dotting with **butter.** Cover and bake in a preheated 375° oven for 30 minutes.

SPINACH (1 box frozen spinach serves 2 meagerly)

Washing fresh spinach is such a chore that you are better off with the frozen. I defy anyone to tell the difference anyhow. Frozen spinach comes plain or chopped. Cook it according to the directions on the box. Put it in a strainer and press the water out of it. Serve plain leaf spinach with **1 tablespoon melted butter** poured over it, with **sliced hard-boiled eggs*** on top, if you like, and with **wine vinegar or lemon juice** on the side.

Put **chopped spinach** in a casserole with **1 tablespoon butter,** a **grinding of nutmeg** and **¼ cup light cream.** Heat. The spinach may be chopped finer before creaming it if you feel, as I do, that it should be. If you like it really puréed, put it in a blender with the cream. Heat with the butter and nutmeg.

STEWED TOMATOES (1 No. 2 can serves 2)

Put **1 slice crustless white bread** in a 250° oven to bake. This will take about 20 minutes.

I'm having you use canned tomatoes here because it's less trouble and the dish is just as good as if you had used fresh.

Put **1 scant tablespoon butter** in a casserole and melt it over moderate heat. Add **1 medium-sized onion,** peeled and chopped. When the onion is golden brown, add

1 can tomatoes, 1 scant teaspoon sugar, a pinch of salt, a pinch of basil and a grinding of black pepper. Lower the heat and simmer, uncovered.

Break the toast into pieces and add it, with a sprig of **parsley**, to the tomatoes. Continue cooking uncovered, over low heat for ½ hour or longer.

TOMATOES STUFFED WITH CORN

Scoop out **2 medium-sized ripe tomatoes** and drain them, letting them sit, upside down, in a colander. Turn on the oven to 350°.

Chop **1 celery heart;** you will need 2 teaspoons chopped celery.

Grate **2 tablespoons Parmesan cheese.** Drain a buffet-size **can whole-kernel corn.** Mix this with the celery and season to taste with **Lawry's Salt** and freshly **ground black pepper.** Fill the tomatoes with the mixture. Melt **2 tablespoons butter** and pour it over the tomatoes. Top with grated cheese. Bake 30 minutes.

SPICY SQUASH CASSEROLE (1 box frozen serves 2)

There isn't room in this small book for me to explore squash as I would like to. Suffice it to say that there are two general kinds of squash, winter and summer, and I'll give you one recipe for each. Winter squash includes acorn, Hubbard and butternut. All of these are fairly similar in taste, and frozen squash, which is usually Hubbard, is so good cooked my way that you might as well string along with that for the time being and forget unfrozen winter squash.

Put the box of **frozen squash** in a colander over a bowl. Do this as soon as you get it home and be prepared for it to sit there for several hours. This is so that it can thaw and much of the excess water can drain away. When you are ready to cook it, which should be about a half to three quarters of an hour before dinner, turn the oven to 300°. Melt **1 tablespoon butter** in a small casserole over moderate heat. Add the squash and **brown sugar** to taste, starting with 1 tablespoon. Add ¼ **teaspoon powdered ginger** and, when the sugar has melted and has been blended with the squash, add **salt** and freshly **ground black pepper** to taste. Keep it hot on an asbestos pad over low heat. Fifteen minutes before dinner, put the casserole under the broiler, watch carefully, and when the squash is nice and brown, remove it and keep it warm in the usual manner.

STEAMED SQUASH (1 pound serves 2)

Summer squash means zucchini, crookneck and the round, white or pale green scalloped type known as pattypan. This kind of squash should be bought young and cooked unpeeled. Pattypan, when small, is cooked whole; the others are cut into 1-inch slices. Steaming is the best way to cook them. Do you remember that I suggested a steamer as part of your equipment?

Wash the **squash** and slice it or not, depending on the kind. Soak it in cold **salted water** for a half hour. Put the steamer in a saucepan big enough to hold the squash. Have water boiling underneath. Don't have any water showing at the bottom of the steamer. Put the squash in the steamer, cover, and simmer for 10 to 15 minutes until the squash is tender. Do not overcook. Lacking a steamer, cook the squash in a small amount of boiling salted water, uncovered. In this case, skip the early soaking. Put cooked squash in a warm serving dish. Sprinkle with **2 tablespoons grated Parmesan cheese** and pour over this **2 tablespoons melted butter.** Don't let the squash wait too long after adding the butter and cheese. The latter will get stringy.

Salads

If a salad is to be any good, everything that goes into it must be nice and cold and the greens must be crisp and utterly free of dirt or sand. Wash lettuce as soon as you get it home, first in hot water and quickly thereafter in very cold water. Allow it to soak in the cold water for a bit. Then shake it dry, to a certain extent, and put it in the crisper compartment of the refrigerator.

Buy the freshest greens that you can find and change the varieties often. For a party and sometimes just for you two, have several different kinds of greens in a salad. You may choose from head lettuce, Boston lettuce, Bibb, romaine, escarole, Belgian endive, watercress and, if you are lucky, sorrel or those lovely narrow little leaves known as field, or lamb's, lettuce. Young spinach leaves may also be used in a salad.

GREEN SALAD

With the exception of Belgian endive and watercress, don't take a knife to salad greens. Cut endive into 1-inch slices or split the head in half lengthwise; cut the stems from watercress and just use the leaves. Separate all other heads of lettuce including, please, the tasteless head or iceberg lettuce (if you must have it) and tear the larger leaves gently with your fingers.

When you are ready to mix your salad, pat the greens dry with a tea towel and put them in a bowl. Pour 1 scant teaspoon dressing per serving into the bowl. Don't overdo it. There should never be a puddle of dressing in the bottom of the bowl. Mix or toss gently with a fork and spoon until each leaf is coated.

If you are putting tomatoes in the salad, wash or peel them, cut them into quarters, and remove seeds and pulp. Place them on a plate in the refrigerator, concave-side down. The remaining juice, which, if left in, would dilute the dressing, will drain out.

Plain sliced tomatoes, with their insides intact, make a very good salad all by themselves. Cover them with French Dressing* and refrigerate for a half hour. This is called "marinating" them.

FRENCH DRESSING

Make a small jar of this and keep it in the refrigerator.

Put **1 teaspoon Lawry's Salt** in the jar. Slice **1 clove garlic** and add it (optional). Add **1 teaspoon paprika** and **¼ cup vinegar**. Change vinegars from time to time; use tarragon, wine, cider or white. Mix with a fork and add **¾ cup olive oil**. Stir and taste. If you like a tarter dressing, add more vinegar. Add herbs if you like, tasting as you go. Take the garlic out of the dressing after 20 minutes. This is important, no matter how much you may like garlic. If the pieces stay in the dressing too long they become stale and the result is a quite horrid taste.

Two or three tablespoons of Roquefort or blue cheese may be stirred into the dressing.

Lemon juice may be substituted for vinegar and should be if you are having wine; vinegar spoils the taste of wine.

SAUCE VINAIGRETTE

To **1 cup French dressing** add **1 teaspoon minced parsley, 1 teaspoon minced chives,** and **1 teaspoon minced cucumber pickles.** A small amount of **chopped hard-boiled egg*** may be added as may **1 teaspoon drained capers.** This sauce is good with cold, cooked artichokes (fresh or frozen), cooked green beans and asparagus (fresh, frozen or canned white).

BEET SALAD

Peel and slice **cooked cold beets** and mix them with **raw onion rings** or **cut-up Belgian endive.** Marinate in **French Dressing*** to which you have added a touch more **vinegar.** Tarragon is the suggested vinegar in this case.

CUCUMBERS IN SOUR CREAM

This is lovely with fish.

☞**HAVE ON HAND**

2 medium-sized cucumbers	dry mustard
½ pint sour cream	white vinegar
1 large Bermuda onion	salt, black peppercorns

Wash and score the cucumbers. That is, take a fork and pull it down the sides of the cucumber, letting the prongs break through the skin. This gives the cucumber slices a pretty scalloped effect.

With a sharp knife, slice the cucumbers very thin. Peel and slice the onion. Put alternate layers of cucumber and onion in a deep bowl, sprinkling each layer with salt and freshly ground black pepper. Pour in enough vinegar to cover, and put the bowl in the refrigerator for several hours. When ready to serve, drain off the vinegar. Mix ½ teaspoon dry mustard with the sour cream and pour this over the cucumbers and onions, mixing thoroughly.

ASPARAGUS AND ARTICHOKE SALAD

Have this on a warm evening with leftover cold chicken or with cold cuts. Serve a hot consommé first and perhaps a Fruit Soufflé* for dessert.

☞ **H A V E   O N   H A N D**

1 No. 2 can white asparagus	1 egg
1 box frozen artichoke hearts	capers or sweet relish
mayonnaise	parsley
tomato catsup	

Hard-boil the egg.* Chill it and mash it with a fork.

Cook the artichoke hearts as directed on the package. Drain and chill. Drain the asparagus and chill.

Make the sauce by combining ½ cup mayonnaise, ¼ cup catsup, the mashed egg, 1 teaspoon drained capers or an equal amount of sweet relish. Arrange the asparagus on cold serving plates, place the artichokes here and there, and cover, or as the pros say, "mask" with the sauce. Sprinkle with chopped parsley.

COLESLAW

There are all sorts of ways to make coleslaw. Here are
three simple ideas on the subject.

Shred ½ **small head cabbage;** that is to say, cut it into
fine strips. Put it in salted ice water to crisp. Drain it
thoroughly and mix it with **French dressing.**°

Or, after draining the **cabbage,** mix it with **½ cup sour
cream** to which you have added **1 tablespoon water,
1 tablespoon vinegar or lemon juice** and **salt** and **sugar**
to taste.

Or mix **¼ cup sour cream** and **¼ cup mayonnaise**
and stir into the **cabbage.**

COOKED VEGETABLE SALAD FOR A BUFFET

This is a fine way to combine vegetable and salad
courses for a buffet. For just two of you, make a half
or a third of the recipe.

☞ **HAVE ON HAND**
      1 medium-sized cauliflower
      1 bunch broccoli
      1 bunch medium-sized or 2 bunches small carrots
      lettuce (Bibb, Boston or romaine)
      French dressing
      salt

Wash and store the lettuce.

Fill three deep saucepans three quarters full of water
and put them on to boil. Add 1 tablespoon salt to each.

Soak the cauliflower and broccoli in cold water. Scrape
the carrots. Remove the outer leaves of the cauliflower
and cut off the stem. Remove tough outer leaves of the
broccoli and cut the stem into 1-inch slices.

When the water is boiling, put the cauliflower in one pan, the carrots in another and the broccoli stems in the third. After the broccoli stems have boiled 5 minutes, add the rest of the broccoli to them. Keep testing the vegetables with a sharp fork and when they are just barely tender drain them and plunge them into cold water. One big pot of cold water will do. Drain them again.

Separate the cauliflower into flowerets and the broccoli into flowerets and small pieces. Cut the carrots into thick pieces or, using the melon ball gadget, make carrot balls. Do this only if the carrots are fairly large. If you were able to find baby carrots, leave them whole. Put each vegetable in a separate dish and pour a small amount of French Dressing* over each. Refrigerate overnight.

To serve, line a bowl or platter with lettuce leaves. Arrange the vegetables on top and sprinkle with a little more dressing.

Peas or green beans may be incorporated in the salad.

RAW VEGETABLE SALAD FOR A BUFFET

I shall generalize here because there are so many variations of this salad.

Eliminate any vegetables you don't care for and add more of another kind.

The day before the party, wash several different kinds of **salad greens.** Wash, quarter, and seed **tomatoes;** wash and seed a **green pepper,** if you like peppers, and cut it into thin strips; wash and slice a bunch of **radishes;** peel, score (run a fork down the sides of), and slice a **cucumber;** wash a nice white **cauliflower** and break it into flowerets; scrape a bunch of young **carrots** and cut them lengthwise into thin strips; wash a bunch of **spring onions** and cut off their beards and an inch or two of the green tops. Put all these vegetables except the onions in a large bowl. Cover with ice water and refrigerate overnight. Wrap the onions in wax paper and refrigerate.

When ready to serve, drain the vegetables thoroughly. Put them in a large serving bowl on a bed of greens. Slice the onions into the bowl. Douse the lot with **French Dressing*** or mix with **mayonnaise** or with **half mayonnaise and half sour cream.**

Desserts

To many people, a meal without dessert is unthinkable; others can take it or leave it alone. For those in the first group, the dessert had better be pretty special, whether it is something light, like a mousse, or something heartier, like apple pie. Others are more easily satisfied; a fruit compote, an ice or a piece of cake will make them happy, and if they don't eat it all or if they just poke at it, no harm is done. I have tried, in this small chapter, to give you a cross section of desserts. Some are easy and some are a little more complicated, but I think that you will find, among them, something to please every taste. In all these recipes "sugar" means granulated sugar, "flour" means all-purpose flour, and "cream" means whipping cream unless otherwise stated.

FROZEN DESSERTS

Many quick, easy and delicious desserts can be made in refrigerator trays or in freezer containers. A mousse is made with whipped cream and needs no stirring. Ices, as you will see, must be stirred and whipped at intervals during the freezing. Generally speaking, all these desserts require about 3 hours in the refrigerator.

FRUIT MOUSSE (4 servings)

Whip **1 pint cream** and fold into it **1 box thawed and mashed frozen strawberries, peaches, raspberries or apricots.** Freeze. Fresh fruit may be used, but it must be mashed and sweetened to taste; ⅓ cup sugar is usually sufficient for 1 cup fresh fruit. One pint fresh fruit approximates 1 box frozen. There must be no largish pieces in the mixture because they will freeze solid. If you only need enough for two, take out half and leave the rest in the tray or container. Don't melt the lot and refreeze some.

MAPLE MOUSSE (2 servings)

Separate **1 egg*** and beat the yolk. Save the white, in a small jar sealed with foil, for later use.

Heat **½ cup maple syrup** and pour it slowly over the egg yolk, stirring. Put the mixture back into the pan in which the syrup was heated, and cook it, stirring, over very low heat until thick. Cool.

Whip **½ pint cream** and fold the maple mixture into it. Freeze, without stirring, in a refrigerator tray or metal bowl.

CHANTILLY MOUSSE (2 servings)

Whip ½ pint cream and add 4 tablespoons confectioners' sugar, a dash of salt, 1 teaspoon vanilla extract and 1 cup crumbled macaroons. Freeze as above.

VANILLA ICE CREAM (2 servings)

Whip ½ pint cream and combine with ½ can sweetened condensed milk to which you have added ½ cup water and 1½ teaspoons vanilla extract. Chill.

VANILLA MOUSSE (4 servings)

Combine ½ can sweetened condensed milk, ½ cup water and 1½ teaspoons vanilla extract. Chill. Whip ½ pint cream and fold into the milk mixture. Freeze as above, but after about 1½ hours, when it is half frozen, turn it into a bowl and beat until smooth. Return it to the refrigerator and freeze it for 1½ hours or longer if necessary. This is like ice cream and will keep, frozen.

ORANGE ICE

This recipe makes 1 quart, but it will keep nicely in the freezer. It's a dandy dessert to have on hand in case of emergency.

Boil together, for 10 minutes, 1½ cups water and ¾ cup sugar. Cool. Add 1 can frozen undiluted orange juice softened just enough so that you can get it out of the can. Freeze it in a refrigerator tray or metal bowl for 3 hours. Stir every hour. Remove from freezer and whip with a rotary beater. Return to freezer for a half hour. Separate 1 egg* and beat the white until stiff (save the yolk). Fold into the orange ice and return to the freezer until ready to use or indefinitely.

RASPBERRY OR STRAWBERRY ICE (2 *servings*)

Wash and hull **1 pint berries**, cover with **½ cup sugar,**
and let stand a half hour. Put them through a food mill
or press them through a strainer lined with cheesecloth.
Add a dash of **salt,** ½ cup water and mix. Taste to see if
more sugar is necessary. Freeze for 3 hours, beating two
or three times during that period.

OTHER DESSERTS

FRUIT COMPOTE, HOT OR COLD

Make a syrup by boiling together **2 cups sugar** and 2
cups water for 5 minutes.

Put **whole fresh peaches** into the syrup and let them
simmer for 1 minute. Take them out and let cold water
run over them. Slip off the skins. If the peaches are not
very ripe, put them back in the syrup and simmer until
tender. Remove and chill for cold compote or keep warm
for hot compote.

Put **pears** in the same syrup and proceed as above.
Do the same with **apricots.** Cook **plums** until they burst
open.

When all the fruit has been cooked, let the syrup
simmer until it is quite thick. If the compote is to be
served cold, chill the syrup, and pour it over the cold
fruit; for hot compote, heat the fruit in the syrup.

Hot or cold fuit, drained of the syrup, may be served
with hot or cold Sabayon Sauce.* Serve the sauce hot
on cold fruit and cold on hot fruit.

SABAYON SAUCE (2 *servings*)

Separate **3 large eggs.** Put the yolks in the top of a double boiler and add **3 tablespoons sugar**. Beat with a whisk or a rotary beater until very light. Add **3 tablespoons Marsala** and mix thoroughly. Have 1 inch of water simmering in the bottom part of the double boiler. Put the top part in place and beat, preferably with a whisk, until the sauce begins to rise and is frothy. If it is to be served hot but you are not quite ready for it, put it in a warm place but not over hot water. Beat it again before serving. If you are having it cold, chill it and beat again before serving. Sabayon is delightful all by itself, poured into tall glasses. It may also be served over fresh fruit.

MACÉDOINE OF FRESH FRUIT

Boil together **1 cup sugar** and 1 cup water for 5 minutes. If you are having **peaches or apricots,** simmer them for 1 minute in the syrup, remove them, run cold water over them, and peel them. Chill the syrup and add **2 tablespoons kirsch** to it.

Slice the apricots and/or peaches and put them in a glass bowl. Wash, pick over, and hull **strawberries** if in season. Do the same with **blueberries or raspberries.** Peel and slice **ripe pears.** Peel and cut a **banana** into slices. Put any or all of these fruits into the bowl with the peaches or apricots and pour the syrup over them. Chill for 2 hours. For fresh fruit with Sabayon,* treat the peaches as above. Pears are also good with Sabayon. If they are not quite ripe, poach them in the syrup before peeling, as in Fruit Compote.*

PEACHES OR PEARS, RASPBERRY OR STRAWBERRY SAUCE

Thaw a box of frozen **raspberries or strawberries** and put the fruit through a food mill or force it through a strainer.

Prepare peaches or pears as in Fruit Compote* or chill and drain **canned Bartlett pears or home-style peaches.** Put the fruit in individual glass dessert dishes and pour the purée over it. A touch of **kirsch** may be added to the sauce. **Whipped cream** may also be added. One box of frozen berries makes enough sauce for 2 generous servings.

CODDLING CREAM (4 servings)

Whip ½ **pint heavy cream** and mix with it ¼ **cup confectioners' sugar** and 1 **tablespoon sherry.** Fold this into 1 **cup applesauce.** Chill. Serve in sherbet glasses, sprinkled with ¼ **cup macaroon crumbs** and a dash of **cinnamon.**

APPLES BONNE FEMME (2 servings)

This is a Gallic glamorizing of the baked apples of your childhood.

☞ **HAVE ON HAND**

2 baking apples	shelled walnuts or pecans
butter	lemon
sugar	apricot jam
seedless raisins	whipping cream (optional)

Preheat the oven to 350°. Put 1 tablespoon seedless raisins to soak in ½ cup warm water.

Core the baking apples without cutting through the stem ends. Be careful to remove all pips. Wipe each apple, but do not peel it. Make cuts here and there in the skin.

Cream (mash together with a wooden spoon in a small bowl) 2 teaspoons butter with 2 teaspoons sugar. Drain the raisins and add them. Chop enough nuts to make 1 tablespoon and add them. Grate enough lemon rind to make 1 teaspoon. Mix that in. Fill the spaces left by the cores with the mixture. Place the apples in a shallow baking dish and add ½ cup water. Bake until tender. This should take about 45 minutes, but sizes of apples vary. Test with a fork after a half hour.

Thin 2 tablespoons apricot jam with 1 tablespoon hot water for each 2 apples. Pour this over the apples and serve hot or cold with or without whipped cream.

BROWN BETTY (2 servings)

This will take him back, and I'll wager it's as good as his mother used to make.

☞ **HAVE ON HAND**

day-old white bread	sugar
2 medium-sized tart apples	powdered cinnamon
butter	cream

Preheat the oven to 350°.

Crumble enough crustless bread to make 1½ cups soft crumbs. Toss them in a skillet, over low heat, with 2 tablespoons butter. Use a fork.

Peel, core, and slice the apples. Butter a 7-inch casserole or baking dish and put in it a third of the buttered crumbs. Cover the crumbs with half the apples and sprinkle with 3 tablespoons sugar and ⅓ teaspoon cinnamon. Cover this layer with half the remaining crumbs and then with the rest of the apples. Sprinkle as before with sugar and cinnamon. Add the remaining crumbs, cover, and bake for 40 minutes. Remove the cover for the last 15 minutes so that the crumbs may brown. Serve with cream.

PRUNE OR APRICOT WHIP (2 servings)

Empty an 8-ounce can of **puréed prunes or apricots** (baby food). Season to taste with **lemon juice** and **confectioners' sugar.**

Separate **1 egg*** and beat the white with a rotary beater until stiff. Save the yolk, with a little **milk** splashed over it, in a small covered dish. Pour the fruit over the egg white and fold in. Serve chilled, in glass dessert dishes, topped with **whipped cream or Custard Sauce.***

CHOCOLATE MOUSSE (2 to 4 servings)

This dessert must be made the day before. Two servings will be generous; four will be meager. Save a little coffee from breakfast for making it.

☞ **HAVE ON HAND**

Baker's German chocolate	vanilla extract
coffee	salt
3 eggs	whipping cream

Cut ¼ pound (4 squares) sweet chocolate into small pieces. Put them in the top of a double boiler over simmering water. As the chocolate melts, add 1½ teaspoons coffee. Stir with a wooden spoon, and when the chocolate has melted completely, remove from the heat.

Separate 3 eggs* and beat the yolks, until light in color, with a rotary beater. Add the egg yolks to the chocolate, beating with the wooden spoon. When the mixture is smooth, add ½ teaspoon vanilla extract.

Add ⅛ teaspoon salt to the egg whites and beat, using the rotary beater, until stiff. Pour the chocolate mixture over the egg whites and fold in. Pour into a glass serving dish and chill overnight. Serve with whipped cream.

FRUIT SOUFFLÉ, CUSTARD SAUCE (4 servings)

As I said earlier, don't be frightened of a soufflé. Perhaps you have already made a cheese soufflé. If so, you know I'm right. If you haven't experimented yet, this is a good one to start on, since it is the easiest of all and has infinite variations. It is made from canned baby food purée, like the apricot whip, and so can have any flavor, including a combination of several. While the recipe is designed for four, two young people can easily put it away all by themselves. If you want to be unselfish, you can serve it when you have just one guest. There is too much sauce for two servings, but that will keep for several days in the refrigerator and is lovely over hot or cold fruit.

☞ **HAVE ON HAND**
    1 can strained baby food purée (4¾ ounces) of any fruit or a combination
    4 eggs
    sugar
    salt
    milk
    flour
    almond extract

First make the Custard Sauce. This may be done in the morning.

Separate 4 eggs* and put the whites aside, covered but not refrigerated.

Put 1½ cups milk in a saucepan, preferably iron, with 3 tablespoons sugar. Heat slowly until bubbles form around the edge of the pan. This is called scalding* the milk. Do not let it boil.

While the milk is heating, beat the egg yolks with a rotary beater until they are light in color; then beat in 1 scant tablespoon flour. Stir a small amount of the hot milk into the egg yolks and then add the egg yolk mixture to the milk, stirring vigorously. Cook, over low heat, stirring with a metal spoon, for 3 to 5 minutes until the sauce thickens and coats the back of the spoon. Turn off the heat but continue to stir, particularly if you are using the iron saucepan. The sauce will continue to cook from the heat of the pan. Pour the sauce into a bowl, add ¼ teaspoon almond extract, and chill. If it should have curdled from overcooking, don't panic; all is not lost. Beat it with a rotary beater. It will smooth out, although it won't be quite as thick.

An hour and a half before dinner, preheat the oven to 325°.

Fifteen minutes later, beat the egg whites until stiff* and when they reach the frothy stage add, while beating, ¼ teaspoon salt and 2 tablespoons sugar. When the whites are standing in glistening peaks, open the can or jar of fruit and empty it over them. Fold it in gently. Don't worry if bits of egg white show. Pour into a 1½-quart soufflé dish, put the dish in a pie tin half full of hot water and bake for 1 hour. Serve with the cold sauce on the side.

CHOCOLATE SOUFFLÉ (2 *servings*)

He will love this. So will you. It only takes 35 minutes to bake, so the thing to do is to make the base at any time during the day. Beat the egg whites and fold them in just before you sit down to dinner. The soufflé will be ready when you are ready for it.

☞ **HAVE ON HAND**
    butter
    flour
    2 eggs
    Baker's chocolate (unsweetened)
    sugar
    salt
    milk
    thick-skinned orange

Preheat the oven to 350° one hour before dinner.

Separate the eggs.* Cover the whites and put them aside but not in the refrigerator.

Put ½ cup milk in a saucepan or measuring cup on an asbestos pad over moderate heat.

Put 1 square of chocolate in the top of a double boiler with ¼ cup sugar and 1 tablespoon hot water from the tap. Have water simmering in the bottom of the double boiler and put the top in position.

Beat the egg yolks with a rotary beater until they are light in color, adding ¼ teaspoon salt while you beat.

In a small iron saucepan, melt 1 tablespoon butter and stir in 1 scant tablespoon flour. Continue to stir with a wooden spoon until smooth. A roux,* remember? Add the hot milk gradually and stir until thick and smooth. Add the melted chocolate.

Stir a little of the hot mixture into the egg yolks; then stir in a little more and then the lot. Mix thoroughly. Add the grated rind of ½ orange and set aside to cool.

Forty-five minutes before dinner, beat the egg whites stiff,* adding a sprinkle of salt while beating. If you have an extra egg white, use it, but be sure that it is at room temperature, as the others are. If you use the extra white, attach a collar to the soufflé dish, as described under Cheese Soufflé.*

Stir a third of the egg whites briskly into the chocolate sauce. Then pour the sauce over the remaining whites and fold in gently. Pour into an unbuttered 1-quart soufflé dish and bake for 35 minutes. No peeking.

Serve with whipped cream or Custard Sauce* to which you have added the grated peel from the rest of that orange.

MERINGUES, PIE CRUSTS AND PIES

I would not advise you to make your own meringues at this time. They are both trying and time-consuming to make, and I suggest that you buy them at a good pastry shop. Get either the kind that are like two halves of a large egg or those that are like nests. Ice cream goes between the two halves or into the nest. Chocolate sauce, which you can buy, is good over meringues and vanilla ice cream; so is a fruit sauce made of thawed and puréed frozen strawberries or raspberries.

CRUMB CRUSTS

Put graham crackers, zwieback or rusks with or without a few gingersnaps on a table and crush them with a rolling pin. For a 9-inch pie you will need **1½ cups of crumbs.** Start with half a box of any of the above and measure as you go along.

Reserving ½ cup crumbs for the top of the pie, mix the rest with **¼ cup confectioners' sugar.** Use your hands. Then stir in, with a wooden spoon, **½ cup melted butter** and a dash of **powdered cinnamon.** Press the mixture evenly on the bottom and sides of a 9-inch pie plate. Chill.

Custard or chiffon pies take nicely to crumb crusts. There are many filling mixes on the market. These will be the simplest for you to make at the moment.

QUICK PIE CRUST (single)

Sift **1⅓ cups pastry flour.** Holding the sifter over a 9-inch pie plate, sift the flour again with **1 teaspoon salt.** In a measuring cup, put **⅓ cup peanut or vegetable oil** and **3 tablespoons milk.** Pour this, without stirring, into the flour in the pie plate. Mix with a fork until blended. Press the mixture evenly, with your hands, over the bottom and sides of the plate. For a baked pie shell, prick all over with a fork and bake in a preheated 425° oven for about 15 minutes or until lightly browned. Otherwise, pour the filling into the pie shell and bake as directed in the recipe.

QUICK PIE CRUST (double)

Sift **2 cups pastry flour;** then sift again with **1½ teaspoons salt** into a bowl. In a measuring cup put **½ cup peanut or vegetable oil** and **¼ cup milk.** Do not mix. Pour it all at once into the flour. Stir with a fork until blended. Press into a smooth ball and cut in half. Flatten halves slightly. Place one half between 2 pieces of waxed paper 12 inches square on a damp table top. This prevents the paper from slipping. Roll the dough out gently to the edges of the paper. Peel off the top piece of paper. If the dough should tear, take a little dab from the outer edge and mend it. Don't moisten it; just press the dab on the torn spot. Lift the bottom piece of paper, with the dough on it, and invert it on a 9-inch pie plate. Peel off the paper and fit the dough gently into the plate. Let the surplus pastry hang over the edges of the plate. Put in the filling.

Roll out the top crust in the same way and place it over the filling. Press the edges of the pastry together with your fingers. With a sharp knife, trim off the excess pastry. Crimp the edges with the prongs of a fork. Cut slits near the center so that steam can escape while the pie is cooking.

For a lattice crust, cut the pastry for the top crust in strips as long as the width of the pie plate and about ¾ inch wide. Weave them over the top of the pie as you would in making a basket. Trim the ends and crimp them with a fork.

APPLE PIE

Make an unbaked 9-inch (single or double) **pie shell** as described above. Fit the pastry into a pan.

Core and peel **5 medium-sized cooking apples.** Be sure that they are tart and crisp. Slice them as thin as you can, and arrange half of them in concentric circles on the pastry.

Mix together **1 cup sugar, ¼ teaspoon ground nutmeg, ¼ teaspoon powdered cinnamon and 2 scant tablespoons cornstarch.**

Spread half of this mixture over the apples. Put the rest of the apples in the pan, again in circles, and spread the rest of the sugar mixture over them.

Melt ½ **stick butter** in 1 tablespoon water. Pour it over the apples. Bake for 1 hour in a preheated 350° oven.

If you wish a top crust, make the double-crust recipe and put the top crust on as directed.

GLACÉED FRUIT PIE OR TARTS

Make a single-crust recipe of **Quick Pastry.** If you want a pie, make it in the pie plate as directed. If you would rather have tarts, make the pastry in a bowl, make a ball of it when it has been mixed, and roll it out between sheets of waxed paper. Take off the top sheet of paper and cut 5 or 6 circle rounds out of the dough. Make the circles a good inch bigger around than the tart pans. Lift them from the paper and fit them into the pans. Bake as directed. Muffin tins may substitute for tart pans.

Wash, drain, and pick over **1 quart blueberries,** or wash and hull **1 quart strawberries,** or peel and slice **enough peaches to make 3 cups.**

Cook ¾ cup berries or ¾ cup peaches in ¼ cup water until soft. Put them through a food mill or force them through a sieve. Add **⅔ cup sugar** and **2 tablespoons arrowroot flour or cornstarch** mixed with ¼ cup cold water. Cook, over medium heat, for a minute or two until the mixture is thick. Chill it and the rest of the fruit separately. All of this may have been done ahead of time.

Whip **1 cup cream.** Sweeten it to taste.

With a slotted spoon, mix the fruit purée with the fruit. Do this gently but thoroughly so that each berry or each piece of peach is coated. Pour into the pie shell

or into the tart shells. Spread with whipped cream or
serve the cream on the side.

LEMON MERINGUE PIE

Most guys like lemon meringue pie and, for that matter,
most dolls do too, so I thought that we had better have
one in the book. This particular one is absurdly easy to
make; try it. Do it early in the day so that it will be
chilled.

☞ **HAVE ON HAND**
      oil and milk (for Quick Pastry*)
      flour
      lemon
      granulated sugar
      salt
      3 eggs
      butter
      confectioners' sugar

Preheat the oven to 350°.
Make Quick Pastry* (single-crust) in a 9-inch pie plate.
Grate most of the outer skin from one lemon. Squeeze
the lemon and strain the juice.
Mix 1¼ cups granulated sugar with ⅓ flour and ⅛ teaspoon salt. Add the lemon juice, reserving 1 teaspoonful.
Add the lemon rind. Mix thoroughly.
Separate 3 eggs.* Do not refrigerate the whites. Beat
the yolks with a rotary beater and stir into them 1 scant
cup cold water. Blend this liquid with the flour-and-sugar
mixture. Pour it into the unbaked pie shell and sprinkle
it with 1 tablespoon butter cut into thin bits. Bake it for

30 minutes. Remove it from the oven and turn up the heat to 475°.

Beat the egg whites with ½ cup confectioners' sugar, added when the whites are frothy. Add that teaspoonful of lemon juice at the same time. Heap this meringue on the pie and bake for 5 minutes until golden brown. Chill.

MINCE PIE

Make **Quick Pastry*** for a 2-crust pie. Add **1 tablespoon cognac** (optional) and **1 tablespoon butter** to the contents of a **1-pound jar of prepared mincemeat**. Fill the pie shell, cover with a full or latticed crust, and bake in a 350° oven for 15 minutes or so, until the crust is golden brown. Serve hot with vanilla ice cream, or with **Hard Sauce** made as follows:

Let **1 stick unsalted butter** soften in a bowl. Cream it, which, as you know, means to mash it with a wooden spoon. When it is smooth and creamy, mix into it **1½ cups sugar.** Most recipes call for confectioners' sugar, but I prefer the crunchiness of granulated sugar. Suit yourself. When the sugar and butter have been well blended, stir in **2 tablespoons Cognac**. Refrigerate until it deserves its name.

PUMPKIN PIE

Canned pumpkin is perfectly satisfactory for making pumpkin pie, and it's much easier to use it than to cook a pumpkin, especially since you have to get such a large one to make enough purée for one 9-inch pie.

Many brands of canned pumpkin have a recipe for pie on the label. Use one, if you like, or try this.

☞ HAVE ON HAND
     1 unbaked 9-inch pastry shell (Quick Pastry*)
     1 No. 2 can or No. 303 can pumpkin
     3 eggs
     ¾ cup sugar
     ½ teaspoon salt
     1 teaspoon cinnamon
     ½ teaspoon powdered ginger
     ¼ teaspoon powdered cloves
     1⅔ cup milk, light cream or half-and-half

Preheat the oven to 425°.

In a fairly large bowl beat 3 eggs lightly with a fork. Add the pumpkin to the eggs and mix them while adding the rest of the ingredients. Pour this filling into the pie shell and bake for 15 minutes. Reduce the heat to 350° and bake until the crust is golden brown and a knife inserted in the center of the pie comes out clean. Chill the pie before serving.

Pumpkin pie is good served with whipped cream or sharp cheddar cheese.

TWO HOMEMADE CAKES

While good cakes can be made from mixes by anyone who can read, and while other good cakes can be bought, it's fun on occasion to make your own from scratch. Here are recipes for two of the most popular cakes. They are easy to make, especially if you have an electric mixer. Try one some rainy day.

FUDGE CAKE WITH CHOCOLATE ICING

☞ HAVE ON HAND
   pastry flour
   double-action baking powder
   salt
   butter
   2 small packages cream cheese (3 ounces)
   granulated sugar
   2 eggs
   milk
   vanilla extract
   Baker's unsweetened chocolate
   confectioners' sugar
   light cream

Preheat the oven to 325°. Butter a regular-sized loaf pan. Soften ¼ stick butter.

In the top of a double boiler, over simmering water, melt 2 squares of chocolate. Mix with 1 cup milk and 1 teaspoon vanilla extract.

Sift 2 scant cups pastry flour and resift, into a bowl, with 2 teaspoons baking powder and ½ teaspoon salt.

Cream the softened butter (mash with a wooden spoon, remember?) until it is very light and add gradually, while creaming, 1 small package cream cheese. If you have a mixer, do the creaming and mixing in that.

After the cream cheese and butter are blended, add gradually, still mixing, 1 cup granulated sugar. Mix in 2 whole eggs, beating vigorously after each addition.

Stir in the flour mixture alternately with the milk-and-chocolate mixture — first a little of one, then a little of the other. Blend thoroughly and pour into the cake pan. Bake for 1 hour. Test with a clean straw from the broom, sticking it into the center of the cake. If it comes out clean, the cake is done. If not, cook it a little longer and test again. When the cake is done, take it out and invert it on a cake rack or on a rack from the oven. Let it stand for 5 minutes and remove the pan.

For the icing, melt 2 more squares of chocolate in the top of the double boiler. Cream the other package of cream cheese and add gradually 2 cups confectioners' sugar mixed with a dash of salt. Stir in the melted chocolate and add just enough cream to make the icing of spreading consistency. Add 1 teaspoon vanilla extract. Spread it on the top and sides of the cake, using a spatula.

POUND CAKE

☞ HAVE ON HAND

butter	milk
granulated sugar	double-action baking powder
4 eggs	vanilla extract
all-purpose flour	lemon, orange

Preheat the oven to 350°. Butter a 10-inch cake or a large loaf pan, about 5 inches by 12 inches. Soften ½ pound butter.

Sift 3 cups of flour into a bowl. Cream the butter and add, while creaming, 2 cups sugar. Add 4 whole eggs, beating after each addition. Then gradually add 2¼ cups sifted flour alternately with 1 cup milk. Stir 1½ teaspoons baking powder into the remaining flour and add to the batter, stirring only until smooth. Add the grated rind of 1 orange, 1 lemon and 1 teaspoon vanilla extract. Pour into the pan and bake for 1 to 1½ hours. Test with a straw as in the preceding recipe. Invert the cake on a rack and remove the pan.

Entertaining

At the beginning of this book I assumed that you didn't know a great deal about cooking. I now assume, as we approach the end, that you have been doing all right. You have mastered some basic techniques and have satisfactorily fed your small family and, on occasion, a friend or two. The time has come to branch out and give a party. But first, where does your groom fit in now that you have come this far along? Perhaps, before we go farther, it's time for

A DIGRESSION ON HUSBANDS

Start getting your husband into the act as soon as you know your way around the kitchen or even before. Let him help you get settled. He'll probably have a better idea than you do about where to put the wall can opener. It's fun to fuss around a kitchen together and, believe me, if you get him interested and involved in this part of your life right from the beginning, you'll never have the sort of

husband who comes home, puts his feet up, and expects
to be waited on. Naturally, there are going to be times
when he is tired or worried and you *want* to wait on him.
For these occasions and, as a matter of fact, just for fun,
have a comfortable chair in or near the kitchen next to
something on which he can put a glass and an ashtray so
that you can visit as dinner is getting cooked. You'll find
that quite often he will say, as you're peeling or chopping
or scraping, "Want me to do that?" Let him.

When it comes to entertaining, you will of course decide together whom you're going to invite. Discuss the
food too. Get his suggestions. If he comes up with something that you feel incapable of doing alone, tell him that
you'll cope with it if he'll help. And don't give him just
the dirty work; let him do something that's fun or chal-
lenging. You'd be surprised how many men are frustrated
cooks and how many could be good ones. They are apt to
be more imaginative and more adventurous in the kitchen
than we are. Give yours his head now and then.

Two things are definitely his department when you
entertain: the outdoor grill and drink mixing. I have not
gone into barbecue recipes; if you have the equipment,
there are many good cookbooks devoted to the subject. As
for drinks, even though he should officiate at the bar for
parties, you should learn to make good drinks too. If he's
busy with the charcoal fire when you're entertaining, you
should be able to take over when a guest needs a refill. Besides, on those evenings of weariness or worry, you should
be able to make his favorite drink and make it just as he
likes it.

There are other things, however, besides drink making
and barbecuing at which your guy could shine. If you go

into the little hibachi business (see below), for instance, he could supervise that, showing people how to go about it, regulating the heat of the fire, and so forth. Perhaps he has ideas about salad and would like to make a ritual of mixing it at the table. Or if you have an electric skillet or a chafing dish, that might be his *expertise* or specialty. The point is that he should be a host in the full meaning of the word and to the same extent that you are the hostess. Neither of you should do it all. I know of instances in which the man of the house invites the guests, plans the menu, shops for the food, and instructs the cook; his wife sits at the head of the table like a beautiful guest. In other families the wife is the whole show and the husband's duties are confined to making the drinks. When there is a man in a white coat to do that, the husband does nothing at all. Don't let yourselves fall into either of these categories. Your parties will be successful if they are the result of a joint effort. It is a rewarding thing to have a husband who is an interested and working partner.

BUFFETS

A buffet supper is the best way to ease into entertaining for a group. Before you decide how many people to invite, look over the seating situation. If you are not setting up card tables, there should be a small table of some sort near each chair so that all your guests will have something handy to put their plates on. If you cannot make more than six people comfortable, invite no more. It's no fun to eat on one's lap.

For the preprandial nibbling, you can get away with salted nuts, interesting crackers and a big bowl of hot popcorn; going to a little more trouble, you can make some of the tidbits mentioned earlier or, if the budget will stand it, you might have shrimp. Another idea is to let your guests cook their own hors d'oeuvres on a Japanese hibachi. Miniature hibachis, called minibachis, are available. They come with a set of toy swords with which people spear pieces of food, grilling them over the charcoal in the little iron pots. On a tray or a tiered plate, all sorts of things can be arranged for them to choose from: cocktail sausages stuffed with cheese and wrapped in bacon, bits of raw lamb or beef that have been marinated in French dressing, dilled plum tomatoes, little meat balls, cocktail onions, etc. This will keep your guests happily occupied if you have last-minute cooking to do — which you shouldn't have.

The meal itself should center around one or two hot dishes that you have prepared long ahead of time and which can be kept hot in chafing dishes or in casseroles on some kind of heater. A big mixed green salad or a vegetable salad should also be on hand. Which it should be depends on whether there are vegetables involved in the main dish. If there are, or if your second hot dish is a vegetable affair, have the green salad. For a warm-weather party you can always fall back on the old stand-bys, cold turkey or ham. As a matter of fact, you can fall back on them, hot, in cold weather; but whenever you do this, make the vegetable or salad unusually interesting.

If you have hot French or Italian bread sliced, buttered and wrapped in a napkin in a basket, you can dispense with butter plates, a sound idea at this kind of a party.

One of my favorite buffet dishes is "strawberries to dunk"; a large bowl of washed but unhulled berries is flanked by smaller bowls holding brown sugar, powdered sugar and sour cream. Guests put a few berries and their choice of sugars and/or sour cream on small plates, and eat with their fingers. A platter of various cheeses, two different pies or a large cake are also good finales for a buffet. Remember that the dessert, as well as the rest of the food, should be easy to eat, not too difficult to cut and not dangerously liquid if you value your carpet. Speaking of carpets, have lots of ashtrays everywhere.

There are several matters which should be attended to a couple of days before a party. It's surprising how many hostesses, even fairly experienced ones, find at the last minute that the best glasses are dusty, the silver platter tarnished, the candlesticks covered with wax, or the napkins wrinkled. Think, well ahead of time, about the dishes, platters, glasses, silverware and linen that you are going to use, and see that they are all ready. Make a careful list of all foodstuffs, including cream for coffee (someone is bound to demand it), and try to have everything on hand that you will need. Even the most devoted husband balks at being sent on too many last-minute errands.

If you are having wine, it should be selected and brought home to rest for a day or two, especially if you are splurging on a good vintage. Wine doesn't like to be drunk before it settles down and gets its breath. When you get it home, put it on its side in a cool dry place away from sunlight. Upend it on the morning of the party day. One hour before serving it, open it so that it can breathe. Chill a white wine. Put a red wine in the room where you are going to dine.

While we are on the subject of wine, let's explore the question of glasses. The glass does not actually affect the

taste of the wine, but the wrong glass *seems* to. Red wine
in a blue glass and white wine in a red tumbler simply
do not taste the way they should. The glasses need not be
expensive, however, and there is no necessity for having
different sizes for different wines. There is an all-purpose
wineglass which not only is correct for any kind of wine
but may also be used for champagne, highballs or martinis.
It is stemmed, tulip-shaped, colorless and holds 8 ounces
or more. When it is used for wine, it should be filled
from one third to one half full, never more. This is so that
you may appreciate the bouquet, which is an important
part of wine drinking.

It's fun to experiment with wine. Get a selection of half
bottles of domestic or imported reds and whites. Imported
wine is not quite as good in small bottles as it is in large
ones, but this is a satisfactory and economical way to find
out what you like. Half bottles of California wines are
always good. Consult with a reputable wine dealer about
your selection. Tell him that you want domestic wines
from premium producers, and be sure, if you are buying a
good imported Bordeaux or Burgundy that it is, in the first
case, "château bottled" and in the second, "estate bottled."
Try some German wine too and, by all means, some inexpensive Italian wines. The latter are perfect for you right
now, when life is simple and appetites are large.

Now, as to what to eat:

HAM JAMBALAYA (*for* 8)

This hearty casserole may be made long ahead of time,
even the day before the party. Take it out of the refrigerator an hour and a half before you want to serve it. Do this

so that it can warm up to room temperature before it goes into the oven.

☞ HAVE ON HAND
 3 pounds lean raw ham cut ½ inch thick
 2 large yellow onions
 garlic (optional)
 2 green peppers
 1 No. 2 can tomatoes
 tomato paste
 beef extract or bouillon cubes
 long-grain rice
 butter
 salt, black peppercorns
 sugar

Cut the ham into bite-sized squares, remove all fat, and reserve it.

Peel and dice the onions; that is slice them and then cut across the slices so that you end up with small bits. Peel and mince 2 cloves of garlic.

Wash the peppers, cut them in half, remove the seeds, and chop fine.

Put 2 cups of water on to boil in a saucepan, and when it does, add 2 teaspoons beef extract (or 2 beef bouillon cubes). Stir and turn off the heat.

Wash 1½ cups rice.*

Put the bits of fat that you trimmed from the ham in a large iron skillet. Turn the heat on to medium and fry (try out) until fat gets crispy and there is grease in the pan. Remove the bits of crisp fat and discard. (If you forgot to read the recipe and threw away the ham fat, use a couple of tablespoons of butter.) Fry the onions and garlic until golden brown. Add the peppers, the can of tomatoes,

1 tablespoon tomato paste and the bouillon. Bring to a
boil, add the rice, and turn the heat down to very low.
Simmer and stir occasionally, using a spatula and turning
the rice completely. If the rice is inclined to stick, add a
little water from time to time.

When the rice is tender, add the ham, saving a dozen
of the prettiest pieces for the top. Add 1 teaspoon freshly
ground black pepper, 1 teaspoon sugar and ½ teaspoon
salt.

Butter a 2-quart casserole and put the ham-rice mixture
in it. Put the extra ham on top. Refrigerate until ready to
bake.

When you have taken the casserole from the refrigerator and warmed it up, put it, covered, in a preheated 375°
oven for 40 minutes. Remove the cover and bake 10 minutes more. Serve from the casserole.

SCALLOPINI OF VEAL (for 8)

This is not a true scallopini, but it's a wonderful and
mysterious dish for a party. Shell the chestnuts the night
before and have your husband help you; it's rough on a
new manicure. A tossed green salad* with tomatoes and,
for a surprise, pickled onions would be a good spicy accompaniment.

☞ HAVE ON HAND
    2½ pounds veal steak cut ½ inch thick
    garlic
    1 pound chestnuts
    peanut oil
    basil
    rosemary
    flour

lemon
cornstarch
salt, black peppercorns
½ pound dried apricots
1 pint sour cream
Marsala wine
butter

Preheat the oven to 475°.

With a sharp knife, make a gash in the flat side of each chestnut. Put the chestnuts in a flat pan with 2 teaspoons peanut oil and set the pan under the broiler for 5 minutes. Remove and, as soon as they are cool enough to handle, crack off the shells and remove the skins with a sharp knife.

Put enough water to cover the chestnuts on to boil. When it boils, add the chestnuts and simmer for 15 minutes. Drain, cool, and cut into fairly big pieces.

Trim the fat off the veal and pound the meat, on both sides, with the edge of your heaviest skillet. Cut the meat into strips 2 inches long and 1 inch wide (approximately).

Mix together ½ cup flour, 2 teaspoons salt and 1 teaspoon freshly ground black pepper. Put this in a paper bag, add the veal, and shake the bag.

Put 5 tablespoons butter or half butter and half peanut oil in a large skillet. Add 1 minced clove garlic. When the butter sizzles, add the meat. Turn the heat down to low and let the meat brown gently, stirring frequently. The pieces won't brown evenly, but that doesn't matter. When they are mostly brown, add ½ cup water and scrape the bottom of the pan with a spatula. Add the sour cream and simmer for a minute or two. Add the chestnuts, 1 teaspoon basil, a pinch of rosemary, 1 teaspoon lemon juice and 5 halves of dried apricots cut into tiny pieces. Add ¼ cup Marsala. Turn up the heat slightly and let the mixture come to a boil.

Put 2 tablespoons cornstarch in a cup and add ¼ cup cold water. Mix and add to the meat. Pour everything into a casserole and sprinkle the top with a few more pieces of dried apricot. The casserole may wait now until 45 minutes before dinner.

An hour before serving, preheat the oven to 350°. In 15 minutes put the casserole, covered, in to bake. The apricot pieces swell up during the cooking and there is a nice mixture of flavors and consistencies.

CALIFORNIA CHICKEN CASSEROLE (for 8)

The perfect accompaniment for this lightly curried casserole is a green bean salad. The cold cooked beans should be tossed with French Dressing* at the last minute, and in this case it would be a good idea to sprinkle the salad with crumbled crisp bacon. In California, mango chutney or spiced peaches are served with the chicken, but regular chutney will do nicely. Always cook long-grain rice by the method in the recipe, using plain water when indicated.

☞ **HAVE ON HAND**
   1 5-6 pound fowl
   stalk celery
   carrot
   parsley
   bay leaf, thyme, salt, black peppercorns
   onion
   dry sherry

butter
1 quart light cream
cornstarch
curry powder
long-grain rice
paprika
Swiss cheese (¼-pound piece)

The chicken may be boiled the day before the party. Put it in a large pot. Wash and store the giblets. Add to the chicken 1 carrot (cut up), 1 stalk celery (chopped), 7 sprigs parsley, 1 medium-sized onion (quartered), and cold water to cover. Bring to a boil, uncovered. Reduce the heat to simmer and "scum" the broth; that is, skim off the fuzz that has accumulated. Season with 1 tablespoon salt, a generous grinding of black pepper, 1 bay leaf and a pinch of thyme. Cover and simmer for 2½ to 3 hours, until the chicken is tender. Let it cool in the broth. Remove it and strain the broth. If this has been done the day before, cover and refrigerate chicken and broth, in separate containers.

The day of the party, wash 1 cup long-grain rice. To do this, put it in a bowl of cold water and rub it between your fingers. Pour off the water and refill with fresh. Rub the rice again. Repeat the process until the water is no longer cloudy. This is tedious, but if you want nice unsticky rice, it's the way to go about it.

Drain the rice and put it in a 2-quart saucepan with 2 cups of chicken broth. If you did not get quite 2 cups of broth, add sufficient water to make up the amount. Add 1 teaspoon salt and bring to a rolling boil. Cover and turn the heat to the lowest possible point. Cook for 14 minutes.

Turn off the heat. Stir gently with a fork. The grains should be separated and fairly tender but not soft for this recipe, since there is more cooking to come. For other dishes, in which tender rice is indicated, allow it to steam, away from the heat, for 5 minutes before removing the cover.

While the rice is cooking, preheat the oven to 400° and grate the cheese.

Skin the chicken and remove all meat from the bones. Cut it into large chunks.

In a saucepan combine 4 ounces sherry, 1 stick butter, 1 teaspoon curry powder, 1 teaspoon paprika and the cream, reserving 2 tablespoons. Dissolve 2 teaspoons cornstarch in the 2 tablespoons cream.

Bring the contents of the saucepan to a boil, reduce the heat to simmer, and stir in the cornstarch and cream. Simmer and stir until thick. Season to taste with salt and ground black pepper.

Put the chicken and rice in a casserole and pour in the sauce. Mix thoroughly. Sprinkle with the grated cheese. Put the casserole in the oven, and when the cheese has browned, reduce the heat to 200° and cook for 45 minutes. Serve from the casserole.

BEEF STEW PAULINE (for 6)

This may not seem very partyish to you, but a group of hungry young people will lap it up if you serve it to them on a fall or winter evening. Have lots of hot bread, several kinds of cheese and a bowl of apples and pears. If the budget will stand some ordinary red wine, so much the better. The stew can be made the day before. If there should be any left over, which is doubtful, it freezes nicely.

☞ **HAVE ON HAND**
  2 pounds lean beef, round or rump, cut in chunks
  1 No. 2 can whole tomatoes
  1 box frozen peas
  6 slender carrots
  smallish yellow onions
  celery
  white bread
  tapioca
  sugar
  salt, black peppercorns
  thyme, marjoram, rosemary

Preheat the oven to 250°.

In a deep casserole, put the meat, tomatoes, peas (uncooked), the carrots (scraped but left whole), 3 onions (peeled and chopped coarsely), 1 cup chopped celery, 2 slices bread (crustless and cubed), 3 tablespoons tapioca, 1 tablespoon sugar, 1 tablespoon salt, a generous grinding of black pepper and pinches of thyme, marjoram and rosemary. If you are going to have red wine, open a bottle and add 2 ounces. This is not necessary. Cover the casserole and bake for 5 hours. Stir a couple of times, towards the end of the cooking. Simple? Good, though.

HAM MOUSSE (for 8)

This final buffet menu is a summer affair. Serve a Vegetable Salad* with the mousse and garnish it, for this party, with hard-boiled eggs,* halved and topped with mayon-

naise. Beer, or white wine and seltzer, or some of each
would be nice to drink. An impressive dessert would be
Macédoine of Fruit* in scooped-out watermelon halves. If
you do this, add watermelon balls to the fruit.

☞HAVE ON HAND
    3 cups ground lean cooked ham
    celery
    green pepper
    capers
    dry mustard
    dill pickles
    parsley
    Worcestershire sauce
    onion
    salt, paprika, cayenne pepper
    gelatin
    chicken broth or bouillon cubes
    dry sherry
    whipping cream
    watercress
    mayonnaise

The mousse must be made the day before the party,
since it must chill overnight.

If you have the butcher grind the ham for you, ask him
to use the coarsest blade. It should really be chopped instead of ground. If you or your beau has the energy, get
out the chopping board and a sharp knife and go to it.

Chop 2 stalks celery and 1 seeded green pepper very
fine. Use the chopping bowl for this. Chop enough dill
pickles, separately, to make 2 tablespoons. Cut enough
parsley to make 2 tablespoons. Mix all these with ½ cup
drained capers, 2 teaspoons Worcestershire sauce and the

ham. Add 2 tablespoons grated onion and 1 teaspoon dry mustard.

Soften 2 tablespoons gelatin in 3 tablespoons cold water. Heat ¾ cup chicken broth if you have some left over. If not, dissolve 1 chicken bouillon cube in ¾ cup boiling water. Combine this with the gelatin. Stir, and when the gelatin is completely dissolved, add ¼ cup sherry and season to taste with paprika and cayenne pepper. Mix with the ham and taste it again. Add salt if necessary.

Whip 1 pint cream and fold* in. Rinse a 2-quart melon mold or two 1-quart bread pans in cold water. Pour in the mousse mixture and chill overnight.

To remove from the mold, run a knife around the sides of the pan or pans. Put it or them in hot water briefly and invert on a cold platter. Garnish with watercress and mayonnaise.

A Short Bibliography

No cookbook writer can pretend to tell it all. As a last addition to your equipment before I leave you, let me recommend the following books, which will enable you to go on beyond the range of this little primer.

The All New Fannie Farmer Boston Cooking School Cookbook (Little, Brown and Company)

The Joy of Cooking by Irma Rombauer and Marion Rombauer Becker (Bobbs Merrill)

The Complete Book of Outdoor Cookery by Helen Evans Brown and James A. Beard (Doubleday)

Massee's Wine Handbook by William Edman Massee (Doubleday)

James Beard's Fish Cookery (Little, Brown and Company)

Season to Taste by Peggy Harvey (Alfred Knopf)

Index

A DIGRESSION ON HUSBANDS,
  163
APPETIZERS AND SOUPS, 37
Apple Pie, 156
Apples Bonne Femme, 148
Apricot Whip, 150
Artichokes, 118
Asparagus, 118
Asparagus and Artichoke Salad,
  139

Baby in the Hole, 19
Bacon, 16
baste, to, 57
Beans, Green or Wax, 119
Beans, Lima, 120
Beef:
  Creamed Chipped, 30
  Crisped Chipped, 37
  Miroton of, 106
  Roast, 52
  Salad Fermière, 107
  Stew Pauline, 175
Beet Greens, 121
Beet Salad, 138
Beets, 120
Boula, 40
Broccoli, 121
Brown Betty, 149
BRUNCHES, LUNCHES AND
  SUPPERS, 14
Brussels Sprouts, 122
BUFFETS, 165
Butter, Maître d'Hôtel, 59
butter, to brown, 51

Cabbage, 122

Carrots, 123
Cake:
  Fudge, Chocolate Icing, 161
  Pound, 162
Cauliflower:
  Au Gratin, 124
  Polonaise, 124
Celery, 125
cereal, remarks on, 15
Cheese:
  Monkey, 34
  Soufflé, 32
Chicken:
  Broiled, 73
  Casserole, California, 172
  Fried, 71
  Gritti, 78
  Livers and Mushrooms, 24
  Roast, 75
Chipped Beef:
  Creamed, 30
  Crisped, 37
Chocolate:
  Icing, 162
  Mousse, 150
  Soufflé, 153
chop or cut, to, 22
Coddle (eggs), to, 28
Coddling Cream, 148
coffee, remarks on, 15
Coleslaw, 140
Consommé Bellevue, 40
Corn, 125
Cornish Game Hen, Roast, 84
cream (butter), to, 149
Cream Cheese Puffs, 38
Croquettes, 113

Crust:
    Crumb, 154
    Quick Pie, 155
Cucumbers in Sour Cream, 138
Curry:
    Ham, 110
    Sauce, 111

DESSERTS, 143
dredge, to, 35
Duck:
    Farmhouse Style, 81
    à l'Orange, 82
    Salmi of, 109
Ducks, Two Roast, 80

egg whites:
    to beat, 21, 33
    to fold in, 24, 154
Eggplant, 125
Eggs:
    Benedict, 26
    Boiled, 28
    Fried, 20
    Hard-Boiled, 28
    Poached, 26
    Scrambled, with Bacon, 16
    Scrambled, with Sausages, 18
    Shirred, 19
    to separate, 23
English Muffins, 27
ENTERTAINING, 163
EQUIPMENT, STAPLES AND
        HERBS, 6

FISH, 86
    Broiled, 90
    Fried, 89
    Poached, 87
    Sautéed, 86
Fondue Neufchâteloise, 35
French Dressing, 137
French Toast, 30

Fruit:
    Compote, Hot or Cold, 146
    Fresh Macédoine of, 147
    Mousse, 144
    Pie or Tarts, Glacéed, 157
    Soufflé, Custard Sauce, 151
Fudge Cake, Chocolate Icing,
        161

Grapefruit, 14
Gravy, Giblet, 77

Ham:
    Curry, 110
    Jambalaya, 168
    Mousse, 175
    Slice, 64
    Spiced Butt, 65
Hamburgers, 102
HERB CHART, 12

Ice:
    Orange, 145
    Raspberry or Strawberry, 146

Jambalaya, Ham, 168

Kidneys, Lamb, 31
KITCHEN EQUIPMENT, 6

Lamb:
    Chops, Broiled, 45
    Hash, Barbecued, 105
    Kidneys, 31
    Mold, 103
    Riblets, Barbecued, 93
    Riblets, Casserole of, 94
    Roast Leg of, 57
    Rolled, Boned Shoulder of, 56
LEFTOVERS, 103
Lemon Meringue Pie, 158
Liver and Bacon, 66
Livers, Chicken, and Mush-
        rooms, 24

Macaroni and Cheese, 101
Macédoine of Fresh Fruit, 147
Maître d'Hôtel Butter, 59
MEAT, HOW TO SHOP FOR, 42
Meat Loaf, 99
MERINGUES, PIE CRUSTS AND
    PIES, 154
Mince Pie, Hard Sauce, 159
Miroton of Beef, 106
Mixed Grill, 47
Mousse:
    Chantilly, 145
    Chocolate, 150
    Fruit, 144
    Ham, 175
    Maple, 144
    Vanilla, 145

Noodles, 31, 80

Omelet:
    Fluffy, 23
    French, 21
Omelets, 20
Onions, 126
    to brown, with roast, 54
    to peel, 48
Orange Ice, 145
Oyster Soup Louisianne, 40

Pancakes and Waffles, 28
parboil, to, 69
Peaches or Pears, Raspberry or
    Strawberry Sauce, 148
Peas:
    à la Française, 127
    and Mushrooms, 127
Pie:
    Apple, 156
    Fruit, Glacéed, 157

Lemon Meringue, 158
Mince, 159
Pumpkin, 159
poach, to, 87
Pork:
    Chops, 60
    Tenderloin, 62
Potato Skins, Baked, 38
Potatoes:
    Anna, 128
    Baked, 129
    Boulangère, 131
    Browned with roast, 54
    Hashed Brown, 130
    Mashed, 128
    Parsley, 129
    Scalloped, 130
    Sweet, 63, 131
POULTRY, HOW TO SHOP FOR,
    70
Pound Cake, 162
PRECEPTS, 3
Prune Whip, 150
Pumpkin Pie, 159
Purée Mongole, 41

Raspberry Ice, 146
rice, to cook, 99, 174
Risotto, 98
Rock Cornish Game Hen, Roast,
    84
Rock Lobster Tails, Broiled, 92
roux, to make a, 32

Salad:
    Asparagus and Artichoke, 139
    Beef, Fermière, 107
    Beet, 138
    Cooked Vegetable, 140
    Green, 137
    Raw Vegetable, 141
SALADS, 136
Salmon Casserole, 91

✽➤❀➤✽➤❀➤✽➤❀➤✽➤❀➤✽➤❀➤✽➤❀➤✽➤❀➤✽➤❀➤✽➤

Sauce:
  Béarnaise, 89
  Custard, 151
  Hard, 159
  Hollandaise, 26
  Mornay (cheese), 79
  Mousseline, 89
  Sabayon, 147
  Verte, 89
  Vinaigrette, 138
  White, 91
  White (thick), 114
  White Wine, for Fish, 88
Sausages, 18
sauté, to, 87
scald (milk), to, 32
Scallopini of Veal, 170
scum or skim, to, 79
sear, to:
  chops, 61
  roast beef, 52
separate (eggs), to, 23
set (roast beef), to, 52
Short Ribs, Braised, with Vege-
    tables, 55
Shrimp:
  in Beer, 38
  Plain Boiled, 39
simmer, to, 26
skim or scum, to, 79
Soufflé:
  Cheese, 32
  Chocolate, 153
  Fruit, Custard Sauce, 151
Soups, 40
Spaghetti and Meat Balls, Scar-
    pellino, 96
Spareribs, 63
Spinach, 132
Squab, Roast, 84
Squash:
  Spicy, Casserole, 133
  Steamed, 134

Staples You Should Have, 9
Steak, Broiled, 49
Steaks, Cubed, 95
Strawberry Ice, 146
Succotash, 120
Sweetbreads, Broiled, 68

Tea, 16
timetable:
  for broiling, 51
  for roasting, 54
Tomatoes:
  Broiled, 48
  Stewed, 132
  Stuffed with Corn, 133
try out, to, 108
Tuna Fish Casserole, 91
Turkey, Roast, 75
Two Homemade Cakes, 160

Vanilla:
  Ice Cream, 145
  Mousse, 145
Veal, Scallopini of, 170
Veal Chops, Maître d'Hôtel, 59
Vegetable Salad:
  Cooked, 140
  Raw, 141
Vegetables, How to Shop
    for, 116

Waffles and Pancakes, 28
Welsh Rarebit, 35
When the Exchequer Is
    Low, 93
Whip, Apricot or Prune, 151
wine, to use in soups, 41
Wines, 168

Zucchini (see Squash, Steamed),
    134